FACING REALITY IN AMERICAN EDUCATION

Why the Racial Gap in Educational Achievement Persists

FACING REALITY IN AMERICAN EDUCATION

Why the Racial Gap in Educational Achievement Persists

Robert J. Walters

TATE PUBLISHING
AND ENTERPRISES, LLC

Published by Tate Publishing & Enterprises, LLC
127 E. Trade Center Terrace | Mustang, Oklahoma 73064 USA
1.888.361.9473 | www.tatepublishing.com

Tate Publishing is committed to excellence in the publishing industry. The company reflects the philosophy established by the founders, based on Psalm 68:11,
"The Lord gave the word and great was the company of those who published it."

Published in the United States of America

ISBN: 978-1-68254-251-4
EDUCATION / Educational Policy & Reform / General
15.08.04

FOREWORD

The plight of America's schools generally and the racial achievement gap in particular have been matters of contention for several decades. As educators have made eliminating the gap their central concern, the overall quality of education given to American children of all races has declined. Yet despite the many efforts—enumerated in this book—the racial achievement gap has remained stubbornly unchanged. It is time for a new approach.

I wish to thank all my friends and supporters, including those who would have preferred I not write this book for fear of personal attacks. Without all the criticism I would not have had the fortitude to stay with this project and gather the information I have over the past 50 years. I can only hope this country has another 50 years to reorient its educational policies according to a more realistic understanding of human nature and human differences.

I wish to dedicate this book to the memory of Dr. Arthur Jensen, professor, scientist, thinker, and courageous defender of the truth concerning human differences and heredity.

—Robert J. Walters

TABLE OF CONTENTS

INTRODUCTION

American educators have long been concerned with the differences in average academic achievement between racial groups. Originally, the issue concerned the failure of black pupils to achieve at the level of whites, but as American society has become more racially diverse, other groups have come into consideration. Today it is customary to distinguish four groups: whites, blacks, Hispanics and Asians. Overall, Asians do somewhat better than whites in school, while Hispanics do somewhat better than blacks; but the gap separating whites and Asians from Hispanics and blacks remains fairly large.

Figure Below: 2000 SAT9 by Ethnicity: Tenth-Grade Percentage at or Above Grade Level (50th Percentile)

African American and Latino Students tend to score well below the score of White students, though White students on average only reach grade level in math and history/Social Studies in grade nine, and in math and science in grade 10.

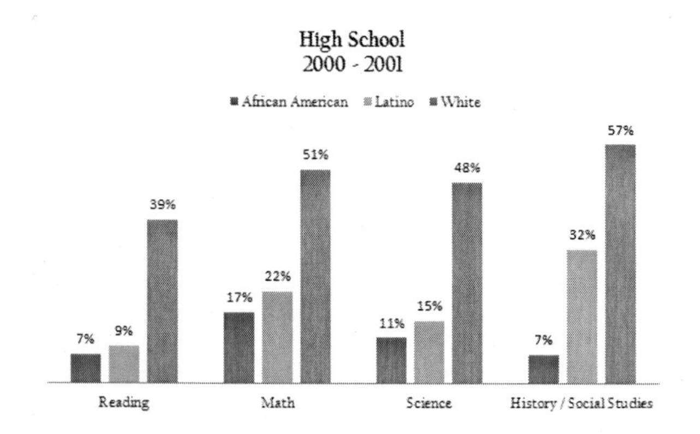

SOURCE: An urban high school, courtesy of Principle Exchange

Index i

Many causes have been proposed to explain all of these differences, and many programs have been implemented in an effort to eliminate them by improving the performance of blacks and Hispanics.

All such efforts have failed; the racial gap has stubbornly persisted. Some blame insufficient funding, some blame achievement tests themselves, some blame the teachers—but nobody has found a solution.

This book explains why the racial achievement gap exists, why it can be expected to continue in the future, and how educational policy makers might best respond to this state of affairs.

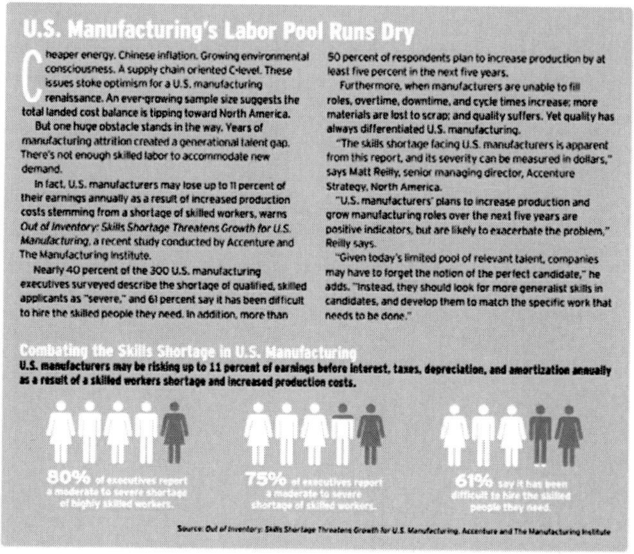

U.S. Manufacturing's Labor Pool Runs Dry

Cheaper energy. Chinese inflation. Growing environmental consciousness. A supply chain oriented C-level. These issues stoke optimism for a U.S. manufacturing renaissance. An ever-growing sample size suggests the total landed cost balance is tipping toward North America.

But one huge obstacle stands in the way. Years of manufacturing attrition created a generational talent gap. There's not enough skilled labor to accommodate new demand.

In fact, U.S. manufacturers may lose up to 11 percent of their earnings annually as a result of increased production costs stemming from a shortage of skilled workers, warns *Out of Inventory: Skills Shortage Threatens Growth for U.S. Manufacturing*, a recent study conducted by Accenture and The Manufacturing Institute.

Nearly 40 percent of the 300 U.S. manufacturing executives surveyed describe the shortage of qualified, skilled applicants as "severe," and 61 percent say it has been difficult to hire the skilled people they need. In addition, more than 50 percent of respondents plan to increase production by at least five percent in the next five years.

Furthermore, when manufacturers are unable to fill roles, overtime, downtime, and cycle times increase; more materials are lost to scrap; and quality suffers. Yet quality has always differentiated U.S. manufacturing.

"The skills shortage facing U.S. manufacturers is apparent from this report, and its severity can be measured in dollars," says Matt Reilly, senior managing director, Accenture Strategy, North America.

"U.S. manufacturers' plans to increase production and grow manufacturing roles over the next five years are positive indicators, but are likely to exacerbate the problem," Reilly says.

"Given today's limited pool of relevant talent, companies may have to forget the notion of the perfect candidate," he adds. "Instead, they should look for more generalist skills in candidates, and develop them to match the specific work that needs to be done."

Combating the Skills Shortage in U.S. Manufacturing

U.S. manufacturers may be risking up to 11 percent of earnings before interest, taxes, depreciation, and amortization annually as a result of a skilled workers shortage and increased production costs.

80% of executives report a moderate to severe shortage of highly skilled workers.

75% of executives report a moderate to severe shortage of skilled workers.

61% say it has been difficult to hire the skilled people they need.

Source: *Out of Inventory: Skills Shortage Threatens Growth for U.S. Manufacturing*, Accenture and The Manufacturing Institute

How severe is your shortage of qualified applicants?

Skilled resource shortage

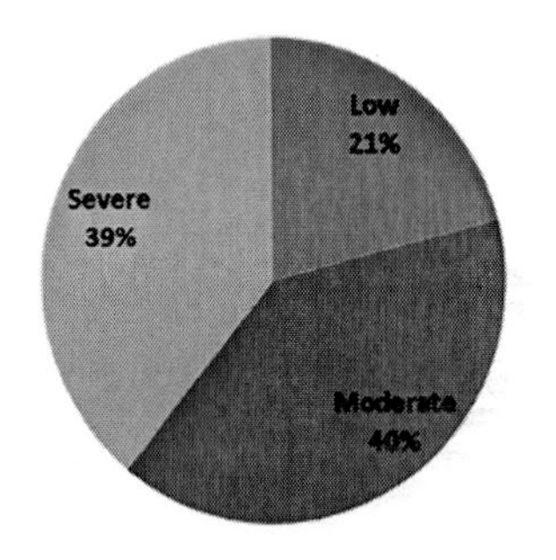

Highly skilled resource shortage

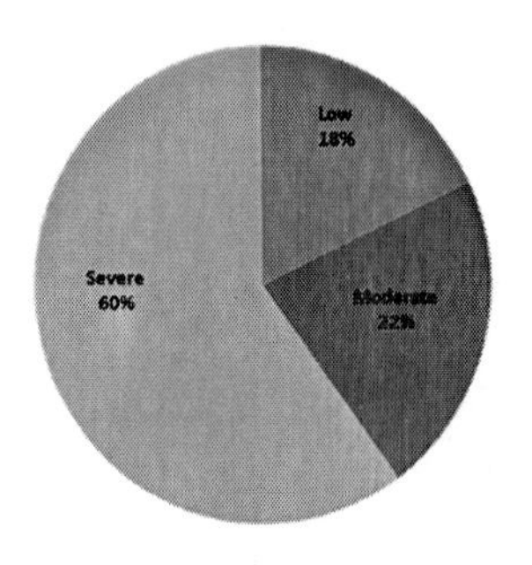

Source: Accenture

Index ii

Why focus on race in a country dedicated to Martin Luther King's vision of a color blind society? In part, because those most dedicated to this vision are themselves the most concerned about the achievement gap, which they see as proof of continuing unequal treatment. More importantly, a study of these differences may lead us to a more realistic, scientifically based understanding of human nature, and to educational policies better adapted to helping children of all races achieve their full academic potential.

In short, this book is meant to offer a different perspective on American education policy, and to suggest changes that might maintain this nation's position as a leader of the free world. Not everyone will agree with my diagnosis or recommendations, but I hope readers will be led to reconsider educational policy options without their vision narrowed with ideological blinders. For the present system is doing a disservice to teachers, to students, and to our country.

Top PISA scores and how the U.S. compares

Country	Math	Rank	Science	Rank	Reading	Rank
Shanghai-China*	613	1	580	1	570	1
Singapore	573	2	551	3	542	3
Hong Kong -China*	561	4	555	2	545	2
Korea, Republic of	554	5	538	7	536	5
Taipei-China*	560	3	523	13	523	8
Finland	519	15	545	5	524	6
Liechtenstein	535	5	525	11	516	12
Switzerland	531	9	515	19	509	16
Japan	536	11	547	4	538	4
Canada	518	14	525	10	523	9
United States	481	35	497	28	498	24

*Test scores and other information for China were reported only for some regions, not for the country itself.

Sources: Organization for Economic Cooperation and Development; Central Intelligence Agency's World Factbook

Index iii

PISA is Program for International Student Assessments and is conducted periodically. This recap was done in 2012.

RACE AND AMERICAN EDUCATION THROUGH *BROWN V. BOARD OF EDUCATION*

Throughout American history, a proper education has always been considered both a desirable goal for the individual and an important benefit to society, but the means to these ends have evolved: from one-room school houses through private, charitable or church-related institutions, to public schools and mandatory attendance laws.

Records indicate that by 1770, private schools existed in all the 13 colonies, though in most places they remained scarce. In the Northern colonies, free blacks were already eligible to attend such schools.

By 1820, separate private schools for whites and blacks had become the usual practice throughout the North, although schools serving blacks were comparatively scarce. Some schools were financed by local governments, some by church organizations, and some by charities.[1] But we should bear in mind that no more

[1] John Hope Franklin, "History of Racial Segregation in America," *The Annals*, March 1956.

than 25 percent of white children received formal schooling at this time; most children of both races were educated informally by their parents. Under the influence of Massachusetts education reformer Horace Mann, non-sectarian public schools proliferated through the Northern States between the 1840s and the Civil War. It was only following the war that the public school system was extended to the South.

After the Civil War, most whites in the South were temporarily removed from the voter rolls during the period known as Reconstruction. Blacks held power in most Southern states at this time, but made no effort to integrate schools. Even after whites regained power in the South, blacks were noted to have received a "relatively fair share of public funds under the promise of Southern politicians to distribute public monies equally."[2]

Toward the end of the nineteenth century, Southern progressives began campaigning for the systematic segregation of all public institutions by race. The Supreme Court gave its blessing to the practice in 1896 when it ruled in *Plessy v. Ferguson* that states could

---

[2] Ambrose Caliver, "Segregation in American Education," *The Annals*, March 1956.

segregate public facilities, including schools, so long as they were "equal."

By 1908, every state of the former Confederacy as well as the four border states had extended their laws to cover segregated schools. There was little black demand for integrated schools at this time; what most blacks wanted was a job and basic education for their children. J. M. Dabbs, e.g., the author of *Southern Heritage*, reported that in the 1890s each race was willing to go to its schools. No less a black leader than Booker T. Washington would say in Atlanta in 1895, "In all things that are purely social we can be as separate as the fingers yet one as the hand in all things essential to mutual progress."

The discriminatory inequalities we so often hear about today began to appear around the turn of the century. In North Carolina, e.g., the ratio of money spent for whites and blacks was practically equal before 1900, with per capita spending on blacks in some years even slightly higher than for whites. However, beginning in 1900–1901 school year, a significant differential in funding began to appear; by 1917, for every dollar spent on the education of black children, whites received $3.08.
This trend met with opposition, however, and spending differentials slowly began to diminish once again. By 1932, per capita expenditure in North Carolina had risen

to $19.40 for whites and $9.24 for blacks. The *Gaines v. Canada* case (1938) held that if a state offered an education for whites, it must offer the same for blacks as well. Many other decisions with the same impact were rendered in the next 14 years.[3]

In 1940, the South's ability to support education (measured in terms of income per school child) was only about half that of the rest of the United States by 1952, the per pupil value of buildings and equipment had increased over 100 percent for whites and 300 percent for blacks. In 1940, 54 percent of the schools for blacks were one-teacher operations; in 1952 the figure had dropped to 10.2 percent. Likewise, the quality of black teachers was improving during these years, and the improvement was reflected in large pay increases. Some states also subsidized education for blacks in subjects not available to them within the state programs.

By 1952, North Carolina was spending $186 for each white student compared to $149.50 for each black student; i.e., the spending gap favoring whites had fallen to 20%. Alabama, Virginia, and the rest of the states with segregated schools followed a similar pattern.

---

[3] A. Rayford W. Logan, "The U.S. Supreme Court and the Segregation Issues," *The Annals*, March 1965.

Funding differentials were predicted to disappear by 1960.[4]

The instruction offered at black colleges was not comparable to that found in white colleges. It was more similar to the curricula of white high schools. Most Americans did not consider this proof of any injustice toward blacks. IQ testing had begun during the First World War, and blacks were found to score on average fifteen points lower than whites. The easier curricula in black schools were widely viewed as a natural and necessary adaptation to the abilities of blacks.

The egalitarian thinking which prevails today first became influential in the 1930s through the efforts of Franz Boas and his followers. Racial egalitarians believed that the lower academic performance of blacks was caused by inferior schools, i.e., schools with fewer resources, poorer teachers and less demanding curricula. They reasoned that if segregation was abolished, and both races offered the same opportunities, they could be expected to achieve the same academic standards.

In accordance with the new thinking, the National Association for the Advancement of Colored People (NAACP) began to push for integration as a tool to improve black performance and thus enhance the

[4] Thomas Woofler, *Southern Race Progress* (Washington, DC: Public Affairs Press, 1957).

position of blacks in America.[5] This campaign culminated in the celebrated case of *Brown vs. Board of Education of Topeka, Kansas*, decided by the Supreme Court in 1954. The immediate point at issue was the desire of seven year old Linda Brown's parents to send her to the school closest to her home, which was white, rather than force her to trek across town to the nearest black school. But much more was involved. In the court's words:

> To separate [children in grade and high schools] from others of similar age and qualifications solely because of their race generates a feeling of inferiority as to their status in the community that may affect their hearts and minds in a way unlikely ever to be undone. Segregation of white and colored children in public schools has a detrimental effect upon the colored children.... for the policy of separating the races is usually interpreted as denoting the inferiority of the negro group. A sense of inferiority affects the motivation of a child to learn. Segregation with the sanction of law, therefore, has a tendency to

---

[5] Some black leaders disagreed. W. E. B. Du Bois broke with the NAACP in 1935 because he felt that they were placing too much emphasis on desegregation, and that "most Negroes cannot receive proper education in white institutions."

> slow the educational and mental development of Negro children and to deprive them of some of the benefits they would receive in a racially integrated school system.

Desegregation was decreed with the express purpose of providing better education for blacks, which would presumably be measurable by improved performance. By this standard, it was a clear failure. The achievement gap between black and white has not grown smaller in the sixty years since the *Brown* decision. Of course, desegregation is still widely celebrated as a great moral triumph. But that is because it is now viewed as an end in itself; the original educational rationale has been quietly forgotten.

The most visible effect of desegregation was that many public schools became *de facto* black schools, as whites moved to the suburbs or transferred their children to private schools. In the South, many new private schools were set up to meet the new demand. The commonest reasons cited were discipline problems associated with blacks and the slower pace of instruction blacks required, which needlessly held white pupils back.

Career and Education: Failure of Counselors to Guide Young Students in America (2014)

Jobs that are not worth the money spent for college:*

	Starting	Mid-Career
Athletic Training	$35,000	$45,900
Medical Training	$47,800	$60,200
Recreation & Leisure	$35,800	$47,100
Secondary School Teacher	$34,500	$46,800
Horticulture	$35,200	$47,700
Nutritionist	$41,700	$56,400
Social Worker	$32,800	$46,600
Theology	$36,800	$51,600
Preschool Teacher	$32,200	$36,400
Administrative Assistant	$33,800	$41,300
Clinical Laboratory	$48,000	$59,900

*Published by Payscale, the creator of the largest compensation database in America

Index iv

EARLY RESPONSES TO THE FAILURE OF BROWN:
BUSING, TITLE I, HEAD START

In many parts of the North, residential housing patterns prevented the Brown decision from having much practical effect. The racial composition of schools reflected the usually unbalanced racial demographics of the neighborhoods where they were located. By the 1960s, many reformers were no longer satisfied with this arrangement. They sought to go beyond desegregation and achieve real integration—racially balanced enrollments—in every school.

In 1963, New Rochelle, New York became the first northern district to close its (single) black school and bus the children to surrounding white schools. There was little resistance. Whites weren't being forced into black schools, and only 850 children were bused out of a total school population of 11,000. While the school administrators admit the test scores of the blacks did not improve, they stressed that there was no evident erosion of white scores either.

The policy of achieving integration through busing received crucial support from sociologist James

Coleman's report *Equality of Educational Opportunity*, published in 1966 and popularly known as the "Coleman Report."

The Coleman Report analyzed 570,000 students from 4,000 American schools. Among its findings was that funding inequities between majority white and majority black schools had disappeared. Most importantly, it argued that black children performed somewhat better in schools where they constituted a minority, but a large enough minority not to feel socially isolated.
Coleman believed the ideal situation was one where blacks made up between 20 and 30 percent of the student body. In such a setting, blacks would escape the effects of socialization in a lower class culture where education was not valued. In Coleman's words, "children who themselves may be undisciplined, coming into classrooms that are highly disciplined, would take on the characteristics of their classmates and be governed by the norms of the classrooms."[6] Encouraged by Coleman's research, some school districts began busing children considerable distances to achieve integration in spite of residential patterns.

By 1968, busing had caught on among educational leaders, and that same year the Supreme Court gave its

---

[6] See Ray Wolters, *Race and Education*, pp. 182-183.

blessing to the practice (*Green vs. New Kent County*). But early results were disappointing, even where busing was accepted by all racial communities. In Hartford, Connecticut, for instance, black and Puerto Rican kids from the "slums" were bused to surrounding school districts as part of Project Concern, inaugurated in 1968. School Director, Thomas Mahan, Jr., later admitted that there was little evidence of the expected academic improvement, but defended the program because it gave minority children a more positive self-image and motivated them to achieve. This turned out to be mistaken; later studies revealed that the self-image of black and Puerto Rican children was harmed once it became clear they could not do as well in tests as their White suburban peers. Residentially based segregation had spared them such invidious comparisons.

Berkeley, California decided in 1968 to integrate its schools completely; but after the first year, results of the "Berkeley Plan" offered few assurances that mixing children racially would achieve the results sought. Attacks by aggressive black gangs in the newly integrated schools left many white parents searching for safer private schools.[7] Test results and teacher comments also indicated that with the elimination of ability grouping, bright students were bored while weaker

[7] *Los Angeles Times*, July 7, 1969

students gave up all effort to learn. Desegregation has produced neither the racial harmony nor the education results once confidently expected.

By the early 1970s, the practice of busing was widespread, despite increasing opposition from parents. When a court ordered the largely black Detroit schools to be consolidated with those of surrounding white suburban areas, the resulting district was so large that some children had to be bused three hours each day! The irony was hard to miss. The original complaint in the *Brown* case had been that segregation forced Linda Brown to travel across town rather than attend her local school; now it was the reformers who were forcing children to travel hours each day in the name of integration. The *Brown* decision had ordered public schools to admit students on a "nonracial basis"; now it was the reformers who were calling for admissions on a racial basis to achieve integration.

By this time, studies were pouring in, and they did not support the view that integration through busing had provided educational benefits for black students. Their scores did not improve, and white students were often harmed by an overall breakdown in discipline and the slower pace of instruction that was necessary to accommodate slow learners. Coleman also came to acknowledge that he had been mistaken. The sample from which he had drawn his conclusions of 1966 consisted of black children who had either chosen to switch to majority white schools or who already lived in majority white neighborhoods. It had been "wishful thinking," he now said, to believe that comparable results could be obtained for all blacks through forced busing.

As evidence of failure mounted, the Supreme Court reversed the lower court ruling that had mandated the Detroit program (*Milliken vs. Bradley*, 1974). The tide had turned, but it took another thirty-three years for the issue to be finally resolved.

In 2000, a longstanding court desegregation order affecting Louisville, Kentucky and surrounding Jefferson County was lifted. The school district, however, voluntarily continued its busing program to insure that between 15 and 50 percent of all school bodies in the district remained black. As elsewhere, this did not narrow the achievement gap. Black high school students trailed their white counterparts by 25 percent in reading and 34 percent in math in an achievement test administered to 9th graders. "We have the most integrated school system in the country," says Carmen Weathers, a retired black teacher. "That sounds good on a business brochure but has nothing to do with education."

In 2002, a parent filed suit on the grounds that her son had been denied admission at a certain school solely because of his race. Her case was upheld by a Supreme Court decision of 2007. Since that time, school districts have been forbidden to assign students on the basis of race even as part of a voluntary effort to achieve integration. Busing was dead. But this decision came more than 40 years after the first studies demonstrating that busing produced no positive results on minority achievement! By this time, over $50 billion had been spent on such operations, about ten percent of the entire educational budget for the districts involved. A good investment? I think not.

Busing to achieve racial balance was not the only effort undertaken during the 1960s to raise black academic performance. The Elementary and Secondary Education Act of President Lyndon Johnson, popularly known as "Title One," was passed in 1965 with the aim of helping the poorest twenty percent of the population (consisting disproportionately of blacks and other minorities) with new schools, equipment and personalized tutoring. The average annual cost of this program was $7.4 billion. By 1999, some $118 billion had been spent, yet University of Michigan, education expert Maris Vinovskis acknowledged that Title I was "a failure up to now." The program has been a failure since then as well, but has never been discontinued. The most recent version formed part of George W. Bush's No Child Left Behind Act. It has never improved the test scores of its supposed beneficiaries, nor has it reduced the achievement gap even modestly.

December 1975 Busing Census

City Population	Charlotte 359,000	Denver 500,000	Pontiac 85,000	Prince George's 700,000	San Francisco 675,000	Tampa 500,00
Average one-way bus trip	30–45 Mins.	20 Mins.	15 Mins.	20 Mins.	15 Mins.	30–35 Mins.
Race Proportions in schools	W-66% B-34%	W-50.7% B-19.1% H-27.2% Other 3%	W-53% B-41% H-6%	W-69% B-31%	W-25% B-30% H-14% A-16% Other-15%	W-80% B-20%
Total Cost of Busing & Size of School Budget	$3.5 million Out of $101 million	$5.5 million Out of $149.5 million	$1.3 million Out of $28 million	$10.1 million Out of $211 million	$4.4 million Out of $160 million	$4.447 million Out of $136.8 million
Students Bused	48,000 Out of 76,000	29,000 Out of 76,500	13,050 Out of 21,000	85,000 Out of 148,000	25,000 Out of 68,000	60,000 Out of 110,000
When Busing Began	1969	1974	1971	1973	1971	1971

Index v

Also launched in 1965 was the highly publicized Head Start program, offering early childhood education and good nutrition to poor children and encouraging parental involvement in childhood education. Originally part of Pres. Johnson's War on Poverty, it is administered by Health and Human Services rather than the Department of Education. As an article in US News put it, "the concept of Head Start is that children from many poor families—hobbled by bad health, a lack of motivation, ignorance about books and even what education is all about—need special aid and guidance to get them ready for school." (22 August 1977)

Early studies seemed to indicate that Head Start was having some success, as children in the program did better in first grade than those who did not participate. But longer term studies indicated that the positive effects diminished quickly over time, sometimes even disappearing by the end of first grade, a phenomenon known as "Head Start fade." Yet the program has been reauthorized each time it has come up for review. In 1981, it was even expanded.

Nearly 30 million children have participated in Head Start through 2014 at a cost to the Federal Government of more than $180 billion (state contributions are also in the billions).

The most rigorous investigation ever done of the program was the Head Start Impact Study, published by the US Department of Health and Human Services in 2010. The experiment began with a representative sample of 4,667 three and four year old children who were randomly assigned either to Head Start or to a control group which did not participate in Head Start. The positive effects of the program were shown to be minimal, and even that minimal effect vanished by the end of the first grade. These results were so shocking that the Health and Human Services (HHS) team sat on them for several years, according to Russ Whitehurst of the Brookings Institution: "I guess they were trying to rerun the data to see if they could come up with anything positive. They couldn't" (*Time*, 18 July 2011). As Andrew Coulson reported, "not a single one of the 114 tests administered to first graders—of academics, socio-emotional development, health care/health status and parenting practice—showed a reliable, statistically significant effect from participating in Head Start." (*New York Post,* 28 January 2010)

In December 2012, HHS released a Third Grade Follow-up to the original study which merely confirmed its findings: participation in Head Start had no statistically measurable effect on any of eleven measures of cognitive ability, including tests of reading, language and math. The debate on the effectiveness of Head Start would seem to be over, yet the program is still being funded by Congress. It recently celebrated its fiftieth anniversary.

Part of the reason for its continuance is that Head Start is really a form of welfare, not education—a child care program for the poor and a patronage program for local Democratic Party honchos (Time Magazine by Joe Klein, July 7, 2011). This is why it is run through HHS rather than the Department of Education. A report issued in 2008 by the New York Academy of Science defends Head Start as money well spent—*not* because of any academic gains, but because it provide jobs and reduces childcare costs for working parents. A senior Obama Administration official recently acknowledged there is some validity to the argument made by opponents of Head Start that it is "merely a jobs program."

As a postscript, we may note the 1995 launch of a program called *Early* Head Start, aimed at preparing two year olds for Head Start. Toddlers in this program can either go to day care centers or receive home visits. The program includes talks with parents about discipline and health issues; mothers are encouraged to read to their kids and not to spank them. Program workers also play with the children to show the mother how to encourage "development."

Efforts are also underway to prepare children for the study of science, technology, engineering and math ("STEM" subjects) beginning shortly after birth. The theory is that the younger they start, the better the chance that they will attend college. Greg Duncan, a professor at UC Irvine who has researched early-childhood education, said children can start learning some STEM concepts soon after birth.

Perhaps educational tapes will some day permit math and science to be taught to fetuses in the womb! Such efforts may contribute no more to academic success than the original Head Start, but they will certainly succeed in destroying the innocent childhood kids used to enjoy before kindergarten.

PARTIAL ROSTER OF ACTIONS TRIED BUT FAILED TO HELP CLOSE THE "GAP"

Address Test Apprehension	Bilingual Education
Black English	Black Teachers for Black Kids
Breastfeed Babies	Calculators for All
College Prep for All	Eliminate Poverty
Equalize All Schools In Money	Forced Busing
Free Breakfasts and Lunches	Grade Inflation to Boost Confidence
Head Start	Higher Teacher Pay
iPads for All	Lead Poising Paint
Longer Day, Less Summer	Lower Test Standards
New Textbooks	Newer Buildings
No Bilingual	Stop Teaching Cursive (Handwriting)
No Memorization	No Structure of Teaching Criteria
Mixing In Every Class	More Money for Schools
On-Line Classes and Video Classes	Pay Students for Success

Pre-School	Quotas for College
Racial Awareness Classes	Segregating Sexes In Classes
Setup Charter Schools	Smaller Classes
Stop Citing Students Who Are Absent Without Cause	Stop IQ Tests
Stop Stereotyping	Stop Suspending Disruptive Kids
Tutoring	Vouchers

THE LAST 60 YEARS OF TRIAL AND ERROR IN THE EFFORT TO CLOSE THE GAP OF ACHIEVEMENT NOT JUST OPPORTUNITY

All these programs failed to bring widespread improvements:

Not Making the Grade.

Despite more investment, U.S. achievement still lags

16:1

Student-to-teacher ratio in 2007 compared with 22:1 in 1970

123%

Increase in per-pupil education spending in the U.S. from 1971 to 2006

0%

Change in academic performance among 17-year-olds from 1971 to 2004 in a national test for reading

89%

Of U.S. Students – 50 Million or so – Attend Public Schools

How do U.S. students compare with students in other developed countries?

5th

U.S. ranking in cumulative K-12 education spending per student in 2006 (only Luxembourg, Switzerland, Norway, and Iceland outspend the U.S.)

21st

Ranking of U.S. students in science literacy out of 30 developed countries in 2006

25th

Ranking of U.S. students in math literacy out of 30 developed countries in 2006

In 2009, 69% of eighth-graders scored below proficient in reading

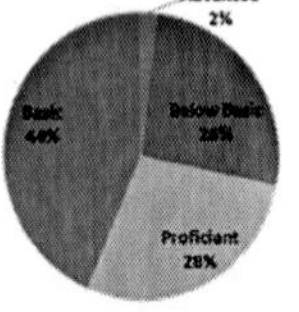

In 2009, 68% of eighth-graders scored below proficient in math

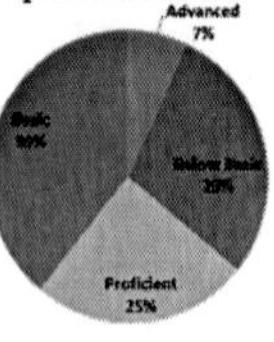

Classes are smaller, and per-pupil spending has increased, but student performance has not improved

Index vi

TRIED AND FAILED TO CLOSE THE "GAP"

The list of initiatives, ideas, and projects that tried to close the education gap between ethnic groups in this country is seemingly endless, but none have achieved significant or lasting success. At best, special attention and all the right factors have led to minor and temporary improvements within limited geographical areas. Let's review some of these initiatives for whatever insight they offer.

MORE MONEY PER PUPIL

Many people believe the cure for most problems in society and the world is more money. Every possible kind and amount of funding for the public schools has been tried somewhere, but without narrowing the race gap and without improving scores generally.

The most lavishly funded public schools in the nation in recent years have been in Washington, DC: $18,677 per pupil in 2010, rising to $27,016 in 2015. If funding per pupil were the key to better education, students in DC should handily outstrip most of their urban peers around the nation. Yet low-income black students in

Washington, DC, are academically behind even other low-income black students in most other cities—in some cases, years behind.

Second to Washington is New York City: $18,618 per pupil in 2010 rising to $21,038 in 2015. Yet nobody would set up New York public schools as a model either. Cambridge, Massachusetts spends 50 percent more per pupil than Boston, just across the river—yet black students in Cambridge lag not only behind whites and Asians, but also behind the state average for blacks and those in Boston.

Black students attending the very integrated neighborhood schools in Shaker Heights, Ohio, have found that moving into middle-class suburbs or achieving middle-class status has not improved their achievement or test scores.

Sausalito School District north of San Francisco is a very wealthy, politically liberal community that has lavishly funded its schools. It ranked number ten among a thousand school districts in California for spending per pupil ($12,000 per student vs. $4,300 in Los Angeles in 1997) and yet most of the white parents have taken their kids out of the school system along with some black parents. Now it is 85 percent black, and all are wondering why more money didn't bring any improvement or success. This is a district that wants for nothing. Art classes, drama instructors, science specialists, computer instructors on all campuses, and class size is 15–20. What else could be the cause, they all wonder?

Stanford University conducted a research project in 2010 by scholars from 32 institutions. They concluded that financial differences among districts "are not clearly related to achievement patterns." But legislators are slow on the uptake; the following year, California gave poor school districts nine percent more money than rich ones!

NEW CLASSROOMS

It has been estimated by one Virginia Tech professor in 2012 that 40 percent of all school buildings need to be replaced. The 21st Century School Fund in Washington, DC, advocates for healthy and safe learning environments. They calculate it would take $271 billion to replace or renovate all schools in America. The assumption here is that old buildings are by nature dilapidated and, therefore, discourage students from learning and teachers from wanting to teach there. This is frequently cited as a reason for the educational gap. So let's see some examples of school construction and what the results have been.

The Los Angeles School District spent $20 billion on new classrooms between 2002 and 2012 (about 20 percent went to unions and overhead). One school, John F. Kennedy High School, was built at a cost of $578 million, the most ever spent to build a school in this nation. In the wake of all this construction, test scores for elementary pupils increased modestly, while high school students suffered a small decline in math scores.
Inglewood, California, has a school district that is in bankruptcy, but which did manage to build a glorious new high school. Test scores did not budge. The same happened in the cities of Oakland, Richmond, and Compton in California. Beautiful new buildings are nice

to look at, but do nothing to diminish the achievement gap.

The most striking effort to lift minority achievement by building new schools came in Kansas City, Missouri in the late 1980s. Judge Russell Clark raised local property taxes from 2.05 to 4.96 percent—the first time in American history that a federal judge has levied taxes—and also ordered the state to hand over funds for the improvement of Kansas City public schools. Other Missouri school districts saw their budgets cut by an average of $250,000 in order to finance the Kansas City program. Within a few years, 418 million dollars had been poured into renovation and new construction in the city. The district got twelve new schools, lavishly equipped with planetariums, Olympic-size swimming pools with underwater observation windows, dust-free rooms for teaching diesel mechanics, at least one mock-United Nations wired for simultaneous interpretation, radio and television studios capable of real broadcasting, video editing and animation labs, a moot court complete with jury room and judges chambers, a model Greek village to teach participatory democracy, elementary schools with one personal computer for every two children, etc. etc. The schools were among the most lavish in the nation. The idea was that such schools would attract white children from the suburbs, and that this would somehow improve the performance of black students.

Every year some 1,400 suburban students took the bus into town to attend the new schools, but the turnover rate was high. A recognizable pattern developed of whites patronizing Kansas City schools only during the lower grades, where the racial performance gap is narrower and blacks less likely to be trouble-makers. By fourth or fifth grade, however, most white children move back to the suburbs or to private schools. In the first seven years of the "desegregation" program, overall white attendance actually dropped slightly, from 26.4 percent to 25.2 percent.

During the same period, the dropout rate rose from 6.5 percent to 11.4 percent, and the attendance rate for seniors dropped from 81.5 percent to 76.2 percent. The racial gap in achievement levels has remained unchanged, starting with a gap of several months in first grade and growing to two or three years by graduation. Test scores on standardized tests—essentially unchanged—are highest in the elementary grades, which have the most whites.

Today's Kansas City schools are 72 percent black. Schools in the white suburbs spend less than half what

Kansas City spends, but student test scores in these suburban schools continue to be much higher.

"We put too much emphasis on trying to attract whites rather than serving the kids that are here," remarks Clinton Adams, a parent activist.

The Kansas City experiment was so radical and its results so clear and unequivocal that it may even convince a few liberals: *no amount of money spent on improving school facilities has bridged the racial gap in academic performance.*

FREE MEALS

Touted as a necessary precondition for learning, the public school lunch program started out small and has mushroomed into the largest food project in America. But does it really help develop skills and increase achievement?

In the early years of the 20th century, school lunches began to be served to children attending public schools in many of America's larger cities. These meals were carefully prescribed by nutrition scientists.

In 1908, for example, the New York School Lunch Committee was founded as a charity to provide 3¢ meals to undernourished kids. These included soups and stew, plus a pudding. By 1912, they were serving 600,000 meals a day. In 1920, their mission was taken over by the Board of Education. By this time, the program's focus had shifted to Americanizing the thousands of immigrant students by providing them with food vastly different from what they were used to at home. It was an effort at assimilation.

When the Great Depression hit, the U.S. Government expanded the school lunch program by directing surplus food to hungry students in order to help them succeed in school. The Federal Surplus Food Corporation setup in

1935 became the focal point of the purchase and distribution of agricultural surpluses (including milk) to schools and certain charities.

President Truman signed the National School Lunch Act (4 June 1946) in response to claims that many servicemen had been rejected during the late war because of diet-related health problems. He argued that "national security" required safeguarding the health and well-being of the nation's children.

In 1966, President Lyndon Johnson signed the Child Nutrition Act of 1966 which established a school breakfast program in public and non-profit private schools. As he said, "good nutrition is essential to good learning."

This program was expanded in 1968 when the Special Food Service Program for Children was created for child care centers and summer programs when school was not in session.

In modern times, vending machines have been added to the mix, and many schools serve food kids like rather than what is best for them: hot dogs, pizza, fried chicken, chocolate milk, etc. They freely accept ethnic foods such as lasagna, chili, and enchiladas. Children tend to eat such foods while avoiding vegetables and other healthy foods. So there has been a strong push by Mrs. Obama and others to make drastic changes in what kids eat. Federal government rules now mandate that certain foods must be served whether they are desired by the students or not. This has resulted in fifty percent or more of the food served each day across the country being thrown out. In Los Angeles schools alone, the waste is said to run to $100,000 per school day.[8] Nationally, the loss is estimated at $1 billion per year. Clearly, today's children are suffering not from insufficient nutrition but from excessive federal mandates on what they are allowed to eat.

Schools and advocates are now looking for a middle road, since federal rules have forbidden realistic changes that would reduce this waste and deliver healthy food that kids will eat.

Today over 9.2 million kids are given free or low-cost *breakfasts*. These are consumed in the classrooms, resulting in much spilt food and garbage, and inhibiting the learning process the meals were meant to enhance. 1.6 million children are also being fed by the public school system over the summer months.

---

[8] *Los Angeles Times*, 5 April 2014

Over half of students attending public schools are eligible for free or reduced-price lunches: 51% according to the Southern Education Foundation (up from 38% as recently as 2000). A majority of children in 21 states are "poor" by the current federal definition. So the Obama administration is asking for $1 billion to subsidize public school meals over the 2016-17 school year. The money is to be funneled to schools with a high percentage of poor students (over and above the billions already earmarked for such students).

Now in Los Angeles Schools, 70,000 *dinners* are being served at 564 schools by the Child and Adult Care Food Program.

It is easy to forget that school meals were originally introduced as a way of assuring proper nutrition to poor (often minority) students in order to raise their level of academic achievement to parity with that of the white, middle-class majority. There is no evidence this has occurred at all.

Some school districts are now providing free lunches to *all* students regardless of need or financial status. This tends to confirm that public school meals no longer have anything to do with insuring proper nutrition with a view to education; they are simply a giant welfare program that allows parents to avoid their responsibilities and provides food producers with a captive market.

UNIVERSAL PRESCHOOL

In North Carolina in 2011, when the state was trying to balance its budget, the legislature reduced by 20 percent what had been a rather large preschool program for low income, at-risk preschool children. This measure was challenged in court on the grounds that the budget cut denied children their constitutional rights. Wake County Superior Judge Howard Manning agreed and demanded that the state pay for continuing the full program no matter what else might have to be cut. He stated, "This case is about the individual right of every child to have an equal opportunity to obtain a sound basic education." He added that each 4-year-old who qualifies for the state program, "is a defenseless, fragile child whose background of poverty or disability places the child at risk of subsequent academic failure."

There is a precedent for judicial mandating of educational programs. In 1998, New Jersey was told by its Supreme Court that all 3 and 4-year-olds in dozens of low-income districts had a right to pre-K, funded by state and district taxes.

But all is not by force. The Pew Charitable Trusts in 2011 finished spending ten years and some $100 million to coax states into expanding and reforming pre-K in 35 states. As a result, an additional 600,000 kids are attending preschool and around 40 percent of 4-year-olds are now in federal or state programs.

Georgia offers a good example of a fully funded, universal pre-K program, and shows us what results can be expected. The state pays for one year of pre-kindergarten classes for *all* kids regardless of background and financial status. But, here again, research shows that the advantages fade by the second and third grades, according to Gary Henry, a policy studies professor at Georgia State University (who has been reviewing the program since 1995).

Leaders in California began pushing for the same widened program in 2006, but with a major twist. As Bruce Fuller (a UC Berkeley professor who opposed a universal plan which was on the ballot that year) said "If we rush toward a universal system and kids from better-off families benefit, we shouldn't expect any narrowing of the achievement gap." So we need, according to him, a discriminatory program that only provides help for the poor. In fact, the *Los Angeles Times* reports in an editorial (18 May 2014) that the gap is getting wider, especially for rich kids who get the best of preschool, lots of books to read, and educational toys to play with. They are pulling ahead of even the middle class, according to Sean Reardon of Stanford's Graduate School of Education.

Congressional hearings in 2013 on the effectiveness of Federal funds for young children found that there are no less than 45 programs in existence, but that none of them produced results which lasted until students were in high school. And then the gap was larger and more pronounced than before any of these programs were started.

Russ Whitehurst, a senior fellow at the Brookings Institution, testified that research showing preschool benefits like increased graduation rates and less time spent behind prison bars is outdated and inapplicable to the large public programs being proposed today. "Preschool has been sold recently as the silver bullet," said Whitehurst, a former researcher for the Department of Education under George W. Bush, "It's not."

RACIAL QUOTAS ("AFFIRMATIVE ACTION")

By 1970, the practice of lowering admissions standards for blacks was gaining strength, encouraged by the federal government. The thinking was that such action was necessary to compensate for the grievous loss of opportunities blacks had suffered under segregation and slavery. Crucially, however, the policy applied not to actual descendents of American slaves, but to blacks *as a race*: blacks newly arrived from Africa or the Caribbean enjoyed all the same preferences.

These policies were gradually extended to other low-performing minorities, with or without historical justification. At present, they apply to all non-Asian minorities, and even to women. The predominant view has come to be that authorities must ensure equal results by race and sex.

Racial preferences can show up in odd places. In 1985, Los Angeles Unified School District ordered the coaches of high school academic decathlon teams to see to it that their squads "reflect the sex and ethnic make-up" of the student body, a requirement that one coach labeled a quota system (he was fired shortly thereafter).

Of course, the policy of racial quotas has always had its opponents. One early critic, San Jose State University President John Bunzel called it unjust and the "worst form of condescension." A liberal Democrat, Bunzel favored certain preferences, but was against outright quotas. "The absolute equalitarians believe that justice requires equality at the end of the race, not in the beginning. We should not make some less equal to make others more equal." He was terminated after this widely reported speech. (February 14, 1975)

Racial preferences did have a large impact on America's graduate and professional schools. As columnist William Raspberry acknowledged (*US News and World Report,* July 24, 1977):

> Between 59 and 70% of blacks in graduate and professional schools would not be there except for special admissions. For medical and law schools specifically, the figures run close to 80%—or as one knowledgeable law professor put it, "Almost all of those not at (predominantly black) Howard University or Meharry Medical College."

Unfortunately, the policies that got blacks into these schools did nothing to improve their performance once they were there.

In Regents of the University of California v. Bakke (1978), the Supreme Court ruled that colleges could consider race as one of several criteria for student admissions, provided they employed no specific numerical quota. Overnight, admissions quota became "goals," and racial favoritism continued much as before. The Bakke case involved a white student, Allan Bakke, who was bumped to allow a less qualified black named Patrick Chavis to take a seat in UCLA medical school. For a time, Chavis became the poster boy for the quota system (dubbed "affirmative action," since the Supreme Court forbade the term "quota"). He was touted by Senator Teddy Kennedy, the *New York Times*, and the *Nation* as the "perfect example" of the success of affirmative action, since he was "serving a disadvantaged community and making a difference in the lives of scores of poor people."

Eventually it became known that Dr. Chavis had made a difference to one Compton, California, community by sending half a dozen of his patients, bleeding and vomiting, to the emergency room—killing one of them.[9]

---

[9] James Webb, *Fields of Fire* (Bantam Books, 2001).

As columnist Michelle Malkin relates:

> Yolanda Mukhalian lost 70 percent of her blood after Chavis hid her in his home for 40 hours following a bungled liposuction; she miraculously survived. The other survivor, Valerie Lawrence, also experienced severe bleeding following the surgery; after Lawrence's sister took her to a hospital emergency room, Chavis barged in and discharged his suffering patient—still hooked up to her IV and catheter—and also stashed her in his home. Tammaria Cotton bled to death and suffered full cardiac arrest after Chavis performed fly-by-night liposuction on her and then disappeared. In 1997, the Medical Board of California suspended Chavis' license, warning of his 'inability to perform some of the most basic duties required of a physician.' In a statement filed by a psychiatrist, the state demonstrated Chavis' "poor impulse control and insensitivity to patients' pain." A tape recording of "horrific screaming" by patients in Chavis' office revealed the doctor responding callously: "Don't talk to the doctor while he is working" and "Liar, liar, pants on fire." (syndicated column of 7 August 2002)

University admissions offices are among the most ruthless practicioners of racial preferences. Both Harvard and the University of Texas at Austin, e.g., have a quantitative procedure for admission decisions, whereby they award 230 extra points to blacks (from anywhere in the world) and 185 extra points to Hispanics; Asians are penalized by having 50 points *subtracted* from their score. All in the name of "equal opportunity," of course. A recent study of affirmative action by the Mellon Foundation and the presidents of eight Ivy League schools reports that minorities who complained about bias got marks no lower than minorities who reported no discrimination. And while encouragement and support clearly helped minorities on campus, the study said, "that race or ethnicity of the helpful faculty members made little or no difference." Again too many hide behind victimhood rather than work hard in the system and do the best they can.

Regrettably, identity politics has become so much an end in itself that beneficiaries of affirmative action are routinely encouraged to focus their studies on the politics of their own racial and ethnic group. It's part of a broader agenda to persuade minorities to focus on their racial identity rather than teaching them practical skills. When first introduced, racial preferences were accompanied by assurances that they would be temporary. This assumed that they would *work*—that they would lead to a situation where they would no longer be necessary. In fact, over the four, going on five decades that this policy has been in place, the racial achievement gap has not narrowed. But instead of seeing this as evidence of failure, supporters cite it as proof of the need to continue the policy of racial preferences indefinitely.

BILINGUAL EDUCATION

American public schools have long had to provide for the needs of students whose first language was not English. The traditional approach emphasized English immersion, with the aim of enabling such students to cope with normal English-language instruction as quickly as possible. This sometimes meant that academic instruction in other subjects had to be put on hold for a time until pupils mastered the English language.

With the aim of helping such students keep up with their peers, the California State Assembly in 1968 passed the Bilingual Education Act, providing for the instruction of non-English speaking students in their own language while they were still mastering English. Most of the students enrolled in the new program were Spanish speakers, but some districts such as Los Angeles have offered bilingual programs in Korean and 67 other languages and dialects. By June 1977, the federal government had spent half a billion dollars in this effort. According to Noel Epstein of the *Washington Post*, there is little evidence that bilingual education has had any positive impact on the achievement level of the students involved. Indeed, a $1.5 million federal study in May 1978 put serious doubts on the value of such programs. It found that 85 percent of the students in them were quite capable of functioning in English-only classes. Critics charge that bilingual education has become nothing more than a jobs program for Spanish-speaking teachers. (page 12)

Responding to such criticisms, the voters in California passed Proposition 227 in 1998 which effectively banned bilingual classes and required students to be taught in English from the beginning. Early results were very positive. Oceanside, California implemented the new law immediately and was surprised at the results that put the students from the 35th percentile to the 45th in one year for the English "learners."

As students struggling with English have moved from the Border States to places like Iowa and New Hampshire, these states have been overwhelmed. Complaints to the Department of Education have been increasing swiftly. The problem is spreading to the entire nation as immigrants, both legal and illegal, seek lower cost housing in other parts of the country.

A 2011 study by the National Center for Educational Statistics showed that Hispanic English learners are falling farther behind Hispanics whose native language is English: 31 points in 2002 to 39 points in 2009. Continued high levels of immigration from Mexico and farther south is eroding the English competence of this demographic faster than English immersion can rectify the problem.

In 2013, the Los Angeles Unified School District (LAUSD) announced plans to segregate English learners from other students for the purpose of English immersion. This is legal, since the basis of discrimination is language competence rather than race; but in fact, the great majority of the students involved are Mexican immigrants. Oddly this new form of segregation was demanded by the US Department of Education, who accused LAUSD of not doing enough for their English learners. It is hoped that this return to English immersion will allow those students to move to the general classrooms within a few years. Some fear it will cause others in the school to feel superior, and this could harm the self-esteem of the English learners. Will any of this work? It is too early to tell.

But as we go to press, an ominous trend is moving in the opposite direction at the state level. Now that the Hispanic population constitutes a majority in California, efforts are afoot to kill Proposition 227 and reinstitute bilingual education, or even education exclusively in Spanish for the entire school career of students who wish it. Such a bill was unsuccessful in the California State Assembly in 2014, but the sponsor has already indicated he will try again in 2015. Demographic trends would seem to make passage just a matter of time.

It has been reported that four high schools teach math and science only in Spanish, using textbooks and computer programs from Mexico. This appears to be illegal, and certainly will not help the students to function in an English-speaking nation.

EBONICS (BILINGUAL EDUCATION FOR BLACKS)

An unusual variant on bilingual education is the proposal that black children be taught through "Ebonics," or black vernacular English. In the summer of 1979, a Michigan judge ruled that a group of black children in the predominantly white Ann Harbor school district had been denied equal educational opportunity because teachers failed to recognize or accommodate their black dialect. Though subsequently overturned, the ruling spotlighted the theory that black children from the lower classes must be taught in their own "language" if they are to reach the same level of achievement as other races. An article in the *Los Angeles Times* (13 January 1986) announced that California was the first state to recognize this and rather than correct those speaking Black English, use it as a springboard for teaching Standard English. It was a kind of "bilingual education" proposal for lower-class blacks. Initial tests indicated that attendance improved, but not student performance.

A bill was even introduced in the California legislature to mandate the offering of classes taught in Black English wherever the student body was more than ten percent black. The bill passed, but was vetoed by Governor George Deukmejian. The strongest resistance to such efforts has come from middle-class blacks, who think it would reinforce stereotyping of blacks.

BUILDING SELF-ESTEEM

The self-esteem movement began in 1969 when psychologist Nathaniel Brandon published a paper called "The Psychology of Self-Esteem." Brandon went so far as to call self-esteem a "key to success in life." Proposals sprang up to spare children negative feedback about their abilities. Even little league baseball stopped keeping score to avoid designating one team the "losers."

This line of reasoning soon crept into the schools. By the mid-1980s, the California state legislature had even created a Self-Esteem Task Force to reform the schools. It came to be thought that a student should pass his class, and perhaps even get a good grade, regardless of his performance.

It soon becomes evident, however, that while self-confidence might help one get a job, it was not so useful for holding one or maintaining a personal relationship. The problem is that boosting self-esteem also boosts narcissism. Thus, the 'me' generation was born. And this generation has a higher likelihood of failing to meet personal career expectations and the lowest career satisfaction. (So says Sean Lyons, co-editor of *Managing the New Workforce: International*

Perspectives on the Millennial Generation.) "We now have a crisis of unmet expectations."

Teachers discovered this in Bessemer School in Pueblo, Colorado. Only 12 percent of the fourth graders there were reading at grade level in 1997. So out went the three hours per week on counseling and self-esteem classes. In came attention to the basics. Up went the test scores. In the fall of 1997, 64 percent of the students passed. And guess what? Self-esteem soared! There is a lesson to be learned here.

A 1975 Stanford University study reported that kids in San Francisco were being killed by kindness. Black and brown kids ranked near the bottom in verbal and math tests, yet these kids had a high regard for their level of education and thought they were working hard at their studies. Sanford Dornbusch, professor in charge of the study, cited: "Blacks think they are working the hardest, but the other evidence shows they are working the least." What we have with the best of intentions is an act of self-delusion. "Praise is negatively correlated with achievement," Dornbusch said. "The lousier the student, the more he is getting praised."

Some earlier studies found that the overt discrimination against minority students was a major factor in their poor performance. But Stanford researchers found "the teachers are saying, 'let's be warm and loving with these kids who arrive with deficiencies.'" The kid is getting love from the teacher, so he thinks he is doing what he is supposed to. They concluded that students need a friendly approach, but with realistic standards and honest evaluations in the process.

Kay Heimowitz reports (Wall Street Journal, August 25,2009) that some 15,000 scholarly articles have been devoted to the study of self-esteem. They demonstrate that high self-esteem does not improve grades, reduce anti-social behavior, deter alcohol drinking or do much of anything good for kids.

> In fact, [she writes] telling kids how smart they are can be counterproductive. Many children who are convinced that they are little geniuses tend not to put much effort into their work. Others are troubled by the latent anxiety of adults who feel it necessary to praise them constantly.

Misplaced self-esteem has done nothing to raise test scores or close the achievement gap. The only real result is a sense of entitlement that has sapped students' will to work hard and accomplish things. Doing something well and being the best you can be is itself the best builder of self-esteem. It doesn't work the other way around.

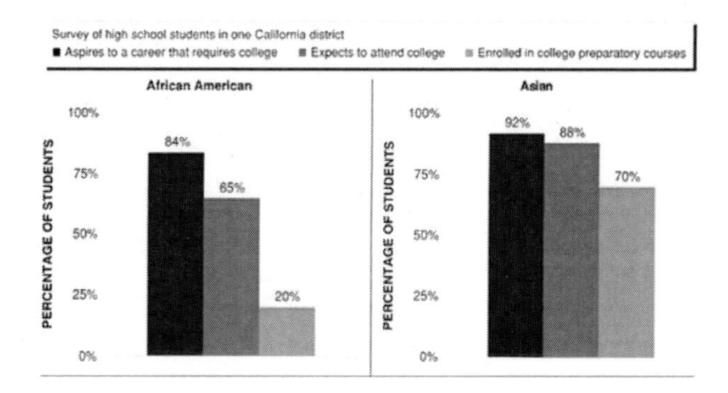

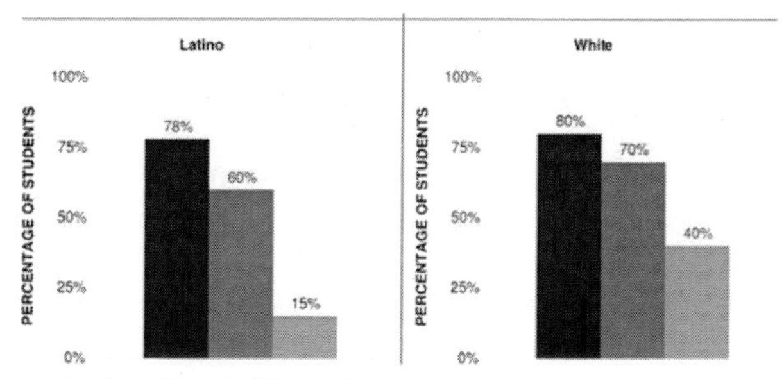

SOURCE: California Department of Education, 1990, Sacramento, CA; The Achievement Council, Los Angeles, CA.

Index vii

SOCIAL PROMOTION

In the late 1970s, as part of the effort to protect students' self-esteem, it became a widespread practice to pass students who were far behind their grade level: simply pushing on through school from grade to grade until they finally "graduated" with little or no usable knowledge. It became known as "social promotion," in contrast to traditional promotion based on achievement. Colleges bore the brunt of the new system by accepting high school graduates who needed massive remedial help even to begin freshman study. Employers, also, found that a high school diploma was no longer any guarantee of an ability to function at work.

A healthy backlash began in Greenville, Virginia. One of the poorest school districts in Virginia, 65 percent black and integrated by means of busing, Greenville ranked in the bottom third on national achievement tests. In 1974, the district announced that they would return to the practice of promoting students solely on the basis of academic achievement. Twice a year, all students would have to take a proficiency test to prove they were at grade level. If they were not, they would not be promoted.

The kids held back are put into remedial classes in reading, writing, and math. Those that cannot or do not want to earn a high school diploma are, at age 14, offered a four year Occupational Proficiency Training Program providing instruction in masonry, mechanics, and other blue-collar trades. They still have to take classes in math and reading, and none can take part in the program without parental permission. They graduate with a certificate that details their job-related skills.
Since the experiment began, the number of students held back, whether black or white, has decreased steadily. At the end of 1974–1975, 630 students were held back, and that dropped to 276 the next year. Achievement test levels rose dramatically, and the drop-out rate was cut in half.

Nonetheless, the NAACP filed discrimination charges against the district on the grounds that those held back were disproportionately black, and that the program therefore amounted to a form of racial discrimination. They also believed the program discouraged blacks from preparing for college by directing them into craft shops for job training. The NAACP thus sued to stop a program proven to be of use to many blacks and some whites.

Since the 1980s, social promotion has been on the defensive, although it is taking a long time to die. At the same time, schools today are coming to realize that simply making students repeat classes they have failed does not accomplish much *unless* they are also offered remedial work in the basics.

In any event, just passing the underachieving kids to the next class neither boosts their morale nor helps them achieve. Holding them back can help them if it is done correctly.

BREASTFEEDING TO RAISE IQ

It has been claimed that the longer babies are exclusively breastfed, the better they do later in life. If this is true, encouraging minority women to breastfeed might reduce the achievement gap.

A study of 1,312 women found no significant correlation between breastfeeding and visuomotor skills or visual memory, but the authors contend breastfeeding does have a lifetime effect on cognitive skills, resulting in a four percent increase in IQ. They claim to have factored in the mother's intelligence level and the amount of in-home stimulation and diet. (*Journal of the American Medical Association of Pediatrics*, 4 August 2013).

A second study conducted by Dr. Bernardo Horta of the Federal University of Pelotas, Brazil, found that "Breast-feeding is associated with improved performance in intelligence tests at age 30 and also has an important effect on societal level by increasing educational attainment and income in adulthood" (*Lanclet Global Health,* 15 March 2015). But Erik Mortensend, commenting on this study in a Danish journal, points out that Dr. Horta's study only demonstrates correlation, not causality; thus, there is no proof that breast-feeding babies causes them to grow up smarter and more successful.

We may also note that virtually all children in Africa are breastfed, yet have the lowest average IQ of any racial group. Black and Hispanic mothers in the US probably—given their economic level—breastfeed more than white and Asian mothers, whose children tend to higher academic achievement.

COMBATING LEAD POISONING

Lead is not good for anyone; this has been known for some time. It has been removed from gasoline, paint, and household items. In the 1960s, doctors diagnosed lead poisoning if blood levels were above 60 micrograms per deciliter. After studies in the 1980s and 1990s, this was reduced to 30, then to 24, then to 10 micrograms, which is about 100 parts per billion. Today doctors use a level of about 3 micrograms.

It is now alleged that even a small amount of lead in children under six can reduce their IQ, and possibly lead to juvenile delinquency and other behavior problems. Researchers writing in the *New England Journal of Medicine* in 2010 estimate that one in 50 children have lead levels that can reduce IQ by up to 7.4 percent. They went on to say that lead is still present in the environment and that it can adversely affect a child.

Influenced by such studies, some persons have proposed that higher exposure to lead may be one reason minority children trail behind whites. Many black and Hispanic families live in older houses more likely to contain lead paint, and there is a tradition in Mexican families of using lead in home cures and ceramic pottery.

But to claim that lead is a major cause of the lower IQ of low-income children and that this explains their lower academic performance is reaching into the sky. If that were true, why have the achievement test levels of black and Hispanic kids not changed in the past 50 years, which have seen lead removed from so many products? The truth is simple. Lead is not healthy, but lead poisoning in now uncommon. In California, e.g., only 21,000 out of two million children tested positively for elevated lead in 2010, or just over one percent. It cannot, therefore, be a core reason for the education gap in various ethnic groups reviewed in this study.

SPECIAL EDUCATION

In 1974, Jack McCurdy, education writer for the *Los Angeles Times*, reported that between two and three times as many minority children were being diagnosed as "retarded" in comparison to whites. This was allegedly due to Anglo, middle-class school authorities mislabeling many minority children. New laws passed that same year demanded that attendance in "special ed" classes not be disproportionate for any socioeconomic class or ethnic group.

Changing the definition of retardation from "under 79 IQ" to "under 70 IQ" did nothing to alleviate the ethnic disproportion.

A Department of Education report issued in June 1993, claimed that white pupils were being diagnosed as "learning disabled," while black pupils were more likely to be diagnosed as "retarded."

In March 2001, the Civil Rights Project at Harvard University ranked states by the racial disproportion of its students in special ed. Blacks are 3.31 times as likely as whites to be classified as mentally retarded in the state, and 2.9 times as likely to be classified as emotionally disturbed. Critics recommended that the Educational

Assessment tests being done in Louisiana be put on hold until "students with disabilities have a chance to learn the material."

Critics also charge that IQ tests are culturally biased, and that this explains why so many low-income and minority kids are diagnosed as retarded.

So programs which are helping thousands of learning-disabled children are under fire because there are allegedly "too many" minorities in this category. But is this going to close the achievement gap or simply help educators pretend it doesn't exist?

PROGRAMS TO HELP FOSTER CHILDREN

It has been alleged that it is more difficult for kids with multiple foster parents, who are frequently being moved from school to school, to focus and learn. In California, there were 43,140 students in foster care as of 2013, and only 37 percent of them were at grade level in math. Foster children as a whole scored lower than all recognized groups, including English learners and special disability kids.

Statewide in California, 58% of foster youths graduated from high school their senior years in 2009-10, compared with 84% in the general population, according to a comprehensive study funded by the nonprofit Stuart Foundation and released last year (*LA Times*, 23 June 2014).

Hispanics make up 43 percent, African Americans 26 percent, whites 23 percent and Asians 2 percent of children in foster care in the state of California. Some allege that the comparatively high number of Hispanic children in foster care is one reason for the achievement gap between whites and Hispanics.

It is difficult to estimate the number before 2013, since privacy laws prevented state education and social service officials from sharing such information. Under a new California state law on equalizing finances for all school districts (taking from the rich and giving to the poor), all districts are now receiving a special stipend of $1,500 per foster student over and above the state mandate of $7,000 per student. School districts are now required to show how the money is being spent in that program, but most have yet to comply (as of 2015).

Santa Ana, California has opened a new high school specifically for foster kids. It currently has only 120 students but is expected to grow to 480. Class sizes are small, and each student receives a computer and is mentored by volunteers. This project is supported by two wealthy men and the Orangewood Children's Foundation. Expectations are high, but it is too early to know whether all this special attention and focus on engineering, technology, science, art, and math will have an impact.

LONGER SCHOOL YEAR

In 2013, forty schools spread across five states and with a total of 20,000 students added 300 hours of instruction to their school years in an effort to "make US education more competitive globally." More than 1,000 schools, including many charter schools, have added hours on their own. In 2009, Education Secretary Arne Duncan even suggested that schools should be open six or seven days a week and should run 11 or 12 months a year. (*LA Times*, 4 December 2012)

Orange County schools in California can better prepare students to compete in a global economy by extending the school year, according to a speech given by William Habermehl, Superintendent of County Schools (24 February 2012). We have heard this message in many other districts around the nation.

The effort to shorten summer vacations received support from a twenty year study by Johns Hopkins University of data tracking the progress of students from kindergarten through high school. They concluded that students made similar progress during the school year, but that better off kids held steady or continued to make progress during the summer, while disadvantaged students fell back. By the end of grammar school, low-income kids had fallen nearly three grade levels behind, and they blamed this on summer time off. Indeed, they allege that by the ninth grade, summer learning loss could be blamed for two-thirds of the achievement gap between income groups.

While this sounds plausible, the facts simply don't support this conclusion. Our students spend more time in the classroom overall yet are far behind most countries in subjects such as math. Many countries have longer school years, but none matches our 6–8 hours per day in class. Korea, Finland, and Japan have out-performed the US on tests, although "they actually spend less time in school than most students in the US" (2011 report by the National School Boards Association's Center for Public Education).

To say that "summer vacation" is the main reason for the gap and its growth as students age flies in the face of all major studies ever done on the subject. Many national studies have suggested that increased time alone does not guarantee higher academic achievement; one good one is *Off The Clock*, by Elena Silva (http://elenamsilva.com/wp-content/uploads/2013/05/OffTheClock2011.pdf). The only group that seems to derive some benefit from extra hours are the low-income English learners who tend to retain what they are taught if they have more time for repetitive study.

MORE BOOKS AT HOME

It has been claimed that if poor and minority families had home libraries and their children read the books or had them read to them at any early age, they would achieve more and the racial gap would narrow. A study carried out at the University of Nevada at Reno indicates that growing up in a home with a five hundred book library correlates with a 2.4 year increase in total schooling. In other countries, the figure is higher, rising to 6.6 years for China. (http://www.sciencedaily.com/releases/2010/05/100520213116.htm)
Of course, this study only demonstrates correlation, not causation; smart parents could be the cause both of more books at home and more schooling for youngsters.

Do parents of any class or race read to their children anymore? Today's children are often addicted to computer play. Living in a house where books sit on a shelf will do nothing for such children. *Reading* books would certainly help them, but there is no proof that even this would raise their achievement scores over the long run. As shown by Head Start, short-term gains often fade with time.

MODIFYING TEXTBOOKS

Since the 1970s, hundreds of special interest groups have attempted to modify or censor the text books used in public schools in order to promote their particular interests or understanding of history. Muslims complain that history books depict them as aggressive and fail to highlight their cultural achievements. Chinese-Americans complain the hardships faced by coolies in building the railroads are not given sufficient attention, atheists do not like the way religion is dealt with, gays want Greek homosexuality given a positive emphasis and Afrocentrists think Rome and Egypt should be portrayed as black cultures.

What most such groups have in common is a desire to downplay the role of European civilization and of America's founding fathers in favor of their own supposedly underrepresented groups. Eliminating Eurocentric stereotypes and biases is one of their stated goals. They believe students from the various groups they champion will achieve more in school if they are presented with positive role models of their own race and books by or about persons like themselves rather than the traditional "white males." They also seek to provide students with a glorified vision of their people's contributions to the world. This, in turn, will supposedly reduce the racial achievement gap. It is one more variant on the theme of self-esteem as the key to achievement.

A typical product of such interest group lobbying is the history textbook *America in Space and Time,* approved for fifth graders as early as 1977. It focuses on biographies of political crusaders such as Martin Luther King, Cesar Chavez and Ralph Nader. The section on slavery is long, with pages of graphic detail, but George Washington is given only one sentence, and no recent president is even mentioned.

More recently, *History Alive* was approved by the California State Board of Education in 1998. This textbook devotes fifty-five pages to Islam, sixteen to Christianity and one to Judaism. The section on Christianity focuses mainly on the Crusades, but without bothering to make clear that they were aimed at recovering previously Christian lands which had been violently overrun and conquered by Muslims.

As textbook "language police" are busy changing novels and textbooks to describe people in gender-neutral terms. Books must portray boys and girls in equal numbers and include "fair" representation of all ethnic groups. "Founding Fathers" is now "Founders," and mention of silos has been removed, since children in ghettos don't know what a silo is. In the novel *Barrio*

Boy, by Ernesto Galarza, the state of California changed "gringo lady" to "American Lady" and "fat boy" to "heavy boy." In New York, references to Judaism are removed from the works of Isaac Bashevis Singer. Stephan Driesler, executive director of the school division of the Association of American Publishers in Washington, DC, responds to criticism by saying "we produce books that the customers want." Joan Bertin, executive director of the National Coalition against Censorship, has summed up the situation well: "Everyone is trying to control the world of ideas, rather than trying to teach students how to think."

Steve Phillips, a San Francisco school district board member, claims "there are studies that show multicultural education does have an impact on the achievement gap of many minority students" (LA Times, 31 March 1998). Unfortunately, he did not specify what studies these are. Nevertheless, he and his colleagues passed a measure requiring that non-whites write more than half the books read by high school students. The "quota" meant teachers have no discretion on the number and nature of the books to be read. The cost of this measure to a district already deep in debt was $2.5 million, but this was seen as unimportant. There is no sign that this reading quota has done anything to improve test scores or achievement levels in San Francisco during the 17 years since the measure was adopted; indeed, scores have dropped and the achievement gap remains as it was.

ETHNIC STUDIES

In 1968, the Black Student Union and a coalition of other student groups at San Francisco State University known as the Third World Liberation Front staged a five month student strike to demand creation of a Black Studies program. They succeeded.

The Black Studies movement quickly spread to universities across America, and spawned imitations such as Chicano Studies and Women's Studies. These programs focus on oppression, identity and the struggle against "dead white males", such as Plato, Aristotle, etc. Today, Yale offers a major in ethnicity, race and migration. Columbia calls their program The Center for the Study of Ethnicity and Race. Farm worker history is taught at UCLA.

In recent years, such courses have been spreading to America's high schools. In the state of California, the El Rancho school district already requires classes in ethnic studies for graduation. Nineteen of 94 senior high schools in LAUSD offer Ethnic Studies, and such courses will be made mandatory beginning with the graduating class of 2017. Originally proposed by School Board Members George McKenna, Steve Zimmer and Bennett Kayser, the LA program aims to narrow the achievement gap between black and Hispanic students and their white and Asian peers. For classes in Chicano Literature and African American History, college credit will be offered.

In 2015, California Assemblyman Luis Alejo, a Democrat from Watsonville, introduced a bill to require ethnic studies at every high school in the state. As we go to press, it appears poised to become the first such law in the nation. California Governor Jerry Brown has promised to sign it.

In Tucson, Arizona, high school Mexican American Studies classes were outlawed in 2010 on the grounds that they were fostering racial resentment and division. The ban received a great deal of national attention, but court rulings have since partially reversed it.

A 2011 study released by the National Education Association(NEA) summarized the need for ethnic studies this way:

> Whites continue to receive the most attention and appear in the widest variety of roles, dominating the story lines and lists of achievements. African Americans, the next most represented racial group, appear in a more limited range of roles and usually receive only a

> sketchy account historically, being focused in relationship to slavery.

The NEA sees ethnic study programs as a way to empower blacks and Latinos and claims that such classes have helped these minorities achieve more and excel more than they would have otherwise. They give no reason why such improvement should be expected; perhaps they are another effort to improve achievement by raising student self-esteem.

We know that Ethnic Studies programs at colleges and universities have done nothing to improve test scores. They often raise grades, however, inasmuch as Ethnic Studies classes are yet notoriously easy. Black Studies departments have even been at the center of academic fraud scandals involving student athletes.

COMPUTERS / IPADS

When I attended high school in the late fifties, adding machines had shrunk to become easily portable and wireless, but our teachers were adamant that we still had to learn the four basic operations of arithmetic: addition, subtraction, multiplication and division. Now caluclators are allowed for performing all basic calculations, supposedly to help students cope with the new electronic world. As a result, young people cannot do simple arithmetic anymore. They need a cash register to tell them how much change a customer is due. Older people are amazed to see young people employ a calculator to multiply by ten.

Computer and internet companies such as ATT, Google, Comcast, and Intel sponsor events like the recent "Digital Learning Day" in California, where educators were bombarded with talk of how the latest digital products will revolutionize education and raise achievement. To help children learn more and take greater interest in their education, computers must be employed in *all* classrooms—so runs the tech industry's less-than-disinterested advice.

Computing devices are not cheap. Los Angeles Unified School District decided in 2012 to provide iPads to all students at a cost of $770 per student, and these devices must be upgraded and replaced every two years. The initial cost to the district was $1 billion in the first year. The money was diverted from a school construction bond, and many were furious at the reappropriation.

Are these machines going to help educate any kids beyond what they could achieve with books? Are they going to help close the achievement gap? It is true that textbooks do get dog-eared and marked on over years of use, but this hardly compares to the beating iPads can get from students (and not just at home). If you drop a textbook, you pick it up. If you drop an iPad, you sweep up the pieces. Many iPads get stolen as well. In three LA high schools it was found that students were able to delete security features and browse the web freely. Such activity can even expose young people to online predators.

The entire purchase program of LAUSD was halted in 2014 after it was learned that the Superintendent conspired to make sure that Apple won the bid against all other companies. Corruption of this sort is likely to get more common, as many school officials are getting elected to office with funding by computer companies.
It was eventually learned that four out of five LA high schools rarely used the iPads at all. Thousands of them simply disappeared!

Despite fiascos like this, authorities such as US Education Secretary Arne Duncan and FCC Chairman Julius Genachowski are still telling us that every school child must have a laptop, because textbooks will soon be a thing of the past. Responding to this declaration, *LA Times* columnist Michael Hiltzik recalled having heard something similar before; he eventually was able to run down this interesting quote from the year 1913: "Books will soon be obsolete in the schools... And our school system will be completely changed in 10 years." (column of 5 February 2012)

Who said this? Thomas Edison. He was speaking of the value of film as a medium of education. His motives may have been no more disinterested than those of computer companies today: more movies in the classrooms meant more money for his company. But a century later, have movies replaced teachers?

Almost every generation since Edison's day has been subjected in its formative years to some "groundbreaking" pedagogical technology. "In the sixties and seventies it was the expectation that TV could revolutionize everything," recalls Thomas Reeves, an instructional technology expert at the University of Georgia. "But the notion that a good teacher would be just as effective on videotape" proved to be unfounded.

And I wonder if Duncan reads his department's own materials? In 2009, the Education Department, which he heads, released a study on whether math and reading software helped boost student achievement in the first, fourth or sixth grades. The study found that the test score difference between those who used software and those who did not "was not statistically different from zero" for the first and fourth grade classes; in the sixth grade, students using software actually got lower test scores—and the effect got significantly worse in the second year of use.

Many would-be educational innovators treat technology as a be-all and end-all, making no effort to figure out how exactly to integrate it into the classroom. Computers are sometimes introduced into classrooms before any actual curriculum has been developed for using them. The truth is that computers are just one more tool in educators' toolkits. How useful they are depends on what educational software is installed, how well the teachers know how to use them, and how well they teach students to use them. If not actively supervised by trained teachers and monitored by parents at home, laptops and iPads become little more than expensive toys.

"Computers, in and of themselves, do very little to aid learning," Gavriel Salomon of the University of Haifa and David Perkins of Harvard observed in 1996. "Placing them in the classrooms did nothing to close the gap in educational achievement since they do not automatically inspire teachers to rethink their teaching or students to adopt new modes of learning." Richard E. Clark, director of the Center for Cognitive Technology at USC, is more blunt: "The media you use makes no difference at all to learning."

Many charter schools in America follow the Waldorf educational philosophy, which prohibits the aid of electronics. Children are encouraged to indulge in free play that nurtures the imagination and interaction with other students; they use no electronic or computer-based educational technology before their teens. Parents of children in Waldorf programs must even agree to prohibit computer games and television viewing at home.

Of course, many parents want their children to learn about computers for the sake of the employment opportunities for which such knowledge will qualify them. The US Bureau of Labor Statistics has, indeed, found that computing occupations are among the fastest growing job categories in the country, and that they pay an average of 75 percent more than the median American salary. And only a small band of kids seem to be moving in this direction—predominantly white and

Asian males. In 2013, 29,555 students took the Advanced Placement computer science exam, but only 18 percent were females, 4 percent African Americans, and 3 percent Hispanics.

According to Jan Margolis and Marcelo Suarez-Orosco of UCLA, many schools and lay persons are missing an important distinction when they consider computer education for our children. Typing, internet play and scanning are not learning about computers for a future vocation. To prepare pupils for entering computer related professions, schools must focus on how computers work and how to program them, not merely on how to use them. Kids surfing the web or doing homework on computers are not developing the critical thinking skills essential to create the software that powers computers. "Students need to learn how to create and produce with technology, not just passively benefit from and consume what has been created by others." (*LA Times* editorial, 20 January 2014)

By this standard, our schools are failing badly according to a report in *Time* magazine August 18, 2014: "Nine out of 10 high schools in the U.S. do not offer computer science.... By 2020, U.S. universities will not be able to fill even a third of the nation's 1.4 million computing positions with qualified graduates."

As the Waldorf educational philosophy reminds us, classroom time spend on computers is time taken away from discussion, debate and collaboration, cooperation, and social interaction. Before we place students into digital cocoons, shouldn't we have them learn how to relate, have empathy for and communicate with others? Shouldn't they be taught how to disagree respectfully, how to defend a point of view, to negotiate and compromise?

There is no evidence that movies, television, videotaped classes or (most recently) laptops and iPads have done anything to improve education or narrow the achievement gap. Yet our leaders have not gotten the message: the latest educational fad, Common Core, requires all participating schools to have computers by the Fall of 2018 and to use them for testing.

Of course, there is nothing necessarily wrong with introducing computing devices to the classroom, but the curriculum should always be determined in advance, the teachers appropriately trained, and the funding source above reproach, i.e., not computer companies or reappropriation of money raised for other purposes.

MANDATORY COLLEGE PREP FOR ALL

Before World War II, only around ten percent of the male population attended college. The other ninety percent were expected to begin work soon after graduating from high school. And within a few years, most such men were able to marry, buy a house, and start a family with a stay-at-home mother—all this with no higher academic credential than a high school diploma. But the postwar years saw an unprecedented boom in college enrollments due to the GI bill. Inevitably, this involved recruiting students farther down the scale of intelligence, including many who previously would have been thought unsuited for college. The level and pace of college instruction had to be adapted to fit the abilities of the new students and in most cases seriously dumbed down.

In recent decades, schools have begun taking this tendency to its logical extreme, succumbing to the notion that *everyone* should attend—or even graduate from—college. Correspondingly, any high school pupil not preparing for college is now seen as a "loser." High schools have gradually eliminated classes in trades such as woodwork, metalwork and auto repair which led to good paying jobs *without* college. Students who might formerly have done well in such jobs are needlessly being made to feel like failures as they are faced with college preparation courses they are neither inclined nor prepared to take.

Blacks and Hispanics both enter college and graduate at lower rates than whites or Asians. Mandatory college prep is now being introduced in some schools with a view to boosting their college attendance in particular. Here are two anecdotes showing how this has played out in California:

1) In 2001, the San Jose school district began requiring all students to pass classes necessary for admission to the California state university system. This change was intended to help more Hispanic students go to college. In 2000, the last year before the mandatory college prep program took effect, 40 percent of San Jose graduates had fulfilled requirements for college.

Early results appeared to show remarkable success, and many people were excited. But all was not as it seemed. It quickly became clear that many students simply could not keep up with college prep courses, so the district was forced to set up an alternative program for them. Fifty percent of these students are Hispanic, the group the college prep system was originally designed to help get into college. The statistics released to the public simply left these students out, making the college prep program appear much more successful than it actually was. Even so, ten years into the program, the percentage of students successfully completing college prep was 40.3, an increase of 0.3 points after ten years of effort.

Hispanic and black students who stayed in college prep still fared worse than others: only 20 percent qualified for college. Dropout rates rose, and many of those who did graduate had a D average that will prevent them from attending college in any case. Yet these young people were made to struggle through college prep courses for their entire high school career rather than taking courses that would be of more practical use for them.

In the final year of the program, 2013, only 34 percent of graduates completed college prep (the decline may have been partly due to the continuing influx of poorly-prepared immigrant students). However, 84 percent of the total student body did graduate from high school in 2013 because most students were excused from taking the supposedly mandatory college prep program. (*Los Angeles Times,* 14 January 2013).

2) Los Angeles schools embarked upon a similar program in 2005 but announced an eight-year transition period. As of 2014, *all* students must have completed a college prep course. A "D" average is acceptable this

year, but by 2017 the minimum grade will climb to a C. That is good enough to get into a college, but is expected to reduce the present 62 percent graduation rate to 16 percent, since 46 percent of those currently passing college prep are doing so with a D average. A *Los Angeles Times* editorial of February 2013 warns us to "Beware of miracles," and pleads for the district to reconsider mandatory universal college prep as a condition for high school graduation: "The proportion of students who qualify for the universities has barely budged over the past decade that these policies have been in place."

Simply forcing all young people to take college prep courses will not bring the percentage of blacks and Hispanics succeeding in college up to the same level as whites and Asians. This is confirmed by every study and analysis done in the past ten years.

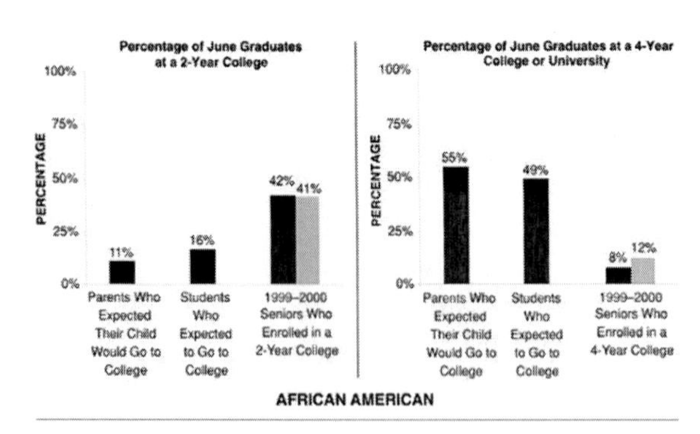

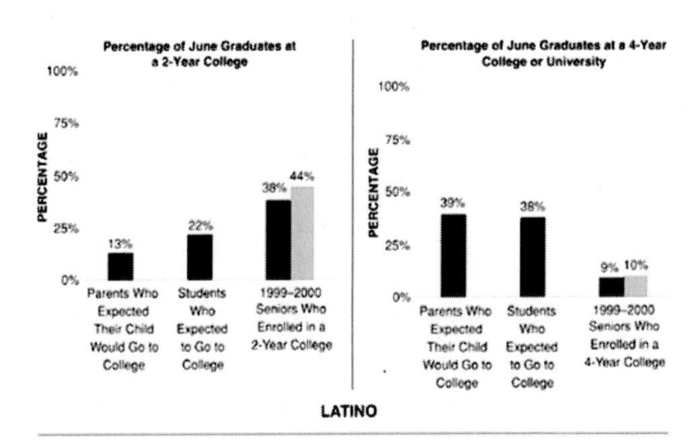
Percentage of June Graduates at a 2-Year College
PERCENTAGE
100%
75%
50%
25%
0%
13%
22%
38%
44%
Parents Who Expected Their Child Would Go to College
Students Who Expected to Go to College
1999–2000 Seniors Who Enrolled in a 2-Year College
Percentage of June Graduates at a 4-Year College or University
PERCENTAGE
100%
75%
50%
25%
0%
39%
38%
9%
10%
Parents Who Expected Their Child Would Go to College
Students Who Expected to Go to College
1999–2000 Seniors Who Enrolled in a 4-Year College
LATINO

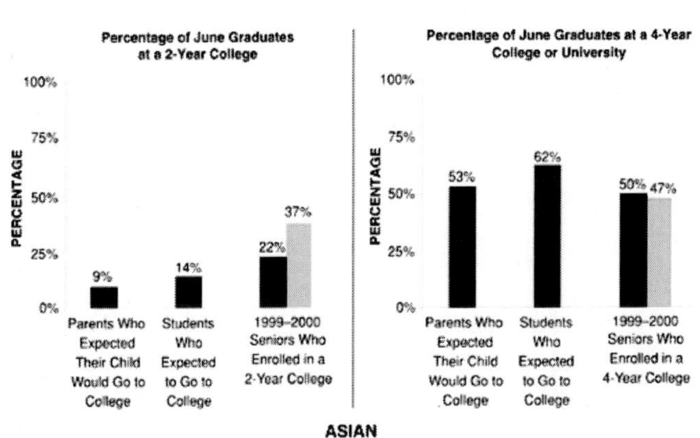
Percentage of June Graduates at a 2-Year College
PERCENTAGE
100%
75%
50%
25%
0%
9%
14%
22%
37%
Parents Who Expected Their Child Would Go to College
Students Who Expected to Go to College
1999–2000 Seniors Who Enrolled in a 2-Year College
Percentage of June Graduates at a 4-Year College or University
PERCENTAGE
100%
75%
50%
25%
0%
53%
62%
50%
47%
Parents Who Expected Their Child Would Go to College
Students Who Expected to Go to College
1999–2000 Seniors Who Enrolled in a 4-Year College
ASIAN

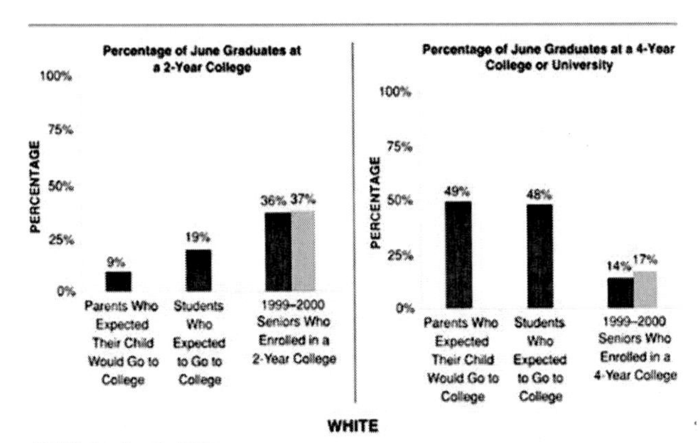

SOURCE: An urban school district.

Index viii

ADAPTIVE EDUCATION (KNEWTON)

The private educational technology firm Knewton, founded in 2008 and based in New York City, promotes the idea that if detailed information on a student can be entered into a personal file that remains open on him during his entire school career (and possibly even into the workplace), this will enable teachers to adapt their approach to each individual student. While this program is intended for all students, its designers hope it will be able to help low achieving and minority students especially, by making it possible for them to be counseled and tutored based on their entire history in the school system.

Teachers traditionally pitch classroom instruction to those of average ability, giving occasional *ad hoc* help for students that need it. Adaptive Learning students in the same math class will go through different sets of lessons as Knewton adapts the material to fit each individual's learning needs and ability. It is a sort of ability grouping within a single classroom. The theory is that the teacher can now teach accurately to the level of each student.

Other, similar programs are now emerging from the geeks in the computer software industry. But we must keep in mind that their advice is not disinterested: the better they can convince schools and teachers to use their systems, the more money they make.

There is also a cost in privacy to this approach, since student records will include details on their family, lifestyle, political and religious beliefs. all in the interest of providing a full picture of the student. This record is meant to travel with the student through school, into college, and possibly even to the job market and the work place. In fact, the information can be turned over to anyone deemed by the authorities to have a legitimate interest in such information, even in the absence of parent approval (US Department of Education directive, 2008). All this is being done with the idea of better helping the individual involved, of course, but the possibilities for misuse should be obvious. The road to hell is paved with good intentions.

Adaptive education also presupposes that teachers have the time to address each and every student's personal mass of data and reports as accrued over their entire school career.

In the seven years of its existence, there is no evidence that Knewton's adaptive education has raised student achievement or narrowed the racial gap.

ONLINE CLASSES

There have been online classes in some form since computers came into common use, but before 2012, they did not enjoy wide acceptance or respectability. The high cost of college today has certainly played a role in shifting opinion. So has massive investment from prestigious universities such as Harvard, Stanford, and MIT. Venture capitalists have taken a keen interest in on-line classes, and the business model is hard to resist. The Udacity company, founded in 2011, is one of the boldest efforts of this type.

Many hoped the low cost and easy availability of such classes would allow racial minorities easier access to a college degree, with all that would mean for their future. Such was the hype that many young people from disadvantaged areas were found to have signed up for one on-line college prep program (Oakland Military Institute) without even having any computer to take the classes!

But the reality has been disappointing. One year after teaming up with Udacity, San Jose State pulled out; most students failed the low-cost classes, far more than failed regular classes.

According to a study done by Public Policy Institute of California, in 2012 about 60% of students enrolled in online courses across the state finished with a passing grade, or about 10% less than the number of students who successfully completed traditional classroom courses. Students under 25, part–time students, Hispanics, blacks and those who needed remedial courses all performed worse in online classes than other groups, according to the report. Racial minorities did much worse than white and Asian students. "We do see the achievement gap exacerbated in the online setting," said Hans Johnson, one of the study's authors.

ADVANCED PLACEMENT

Advanced Placement classes have been around since 1955, allowing qualified high school students to take college level classes and get college credit. They were originally designed to keep bright students interested and working at their full potential. But they have evolved into a way for any student—even a poor student—to play the college admissions game.

As former history teacher Brian Gibbs has written in the *Los Angeles Times*:

> When the Times reported that the number of Advanced Placement exams taken in the Los Angeles Unified School District had hit an all-time high, I couldn't help but wonder: Is that a good thing? AP courses help high school students gain admission to prestigious colleges, but not necessarily because of the course work. What matters is getting the AP course on the transcript. AP classes are really a numbers racket: most colleges reward applicants for taking AP courses, the more the better. (13 August 2014)

Four days after this article appeared, it was announced that California has received $10.7 million from the US Department of Education to prepare low-income and "underserved" high school students by covering the costs of advanced course tests that can run up to $89. In 2014 $28.4 million in grants were issued nationwide, with funding levels determined by the number of *low-income* students expected to take the exams. AP has evolved from a program for high-achievers to just another attempt at uplifting the poor (disproportionately blacks and Hispanics). By subsidizing AP tests for the poor, the authorities hope to get more black and Hispanic students into college.

In Los Angeles Unified School District, The number of AP tests being taken in Los Angeles is, accordingly, rising: 48,000 in 2013–14, up 62 percent from seven years earlier. And yet, the stress on low income students has not improved their performance relative to middle- and high-income students; nor has the racial achievement gap gotten narrower.

MORE EDUCATION FOR TEACHERS

Another theory is that our teachers would do a better job if they themselves got more education, and the gap would become a thing of the past.

It is true that American teachers tend not to be high achievers. In 2010, half graduated in the bottom third of their class (*Time*, 14 November 2011). But it is also important to understand just what is meant by "education" in America's teachers' colleges. In a 1998 article, John Leo reported that prospective teachers at the University of Massachusetts, Amherst, were being offered courses such as: "Social Diversity in Education", "Embracing Diversity", "Diversity and Change", "Oppression and Education", "Introduction to Multicultural Education", "Black Identity", "Classism", "Racism", "Sexism", "Jewish Oppression", "Lesbian / Gay / Bisexual Oppression", "Oppression of the Disabled" and "Erroneous Beliefs."

As one of Leo's readers commented, "This explains why 59 percent of our prospective teachers in this state flunked a basic literacy test."

This 59 percent failure rate occurred with 1,800 prospective teachers who took a tenth-grade test in math and language. As Leo remarks, "Apparently they went into ed school without knowing much about anything, then came out the same way. But at least they are prepared to drill children in separatism, oppression and erroneous beliefs."

> Conservatives talk about striving and standards, liberals talk about equal funding and classroom size, but few talk about the breeding grounds for school failure—the trendy, anti-achievement, oppression-obsessed, feel-good, esteem-ridden, content-free schools of education [Ed schools] teach nothing about anything in the real world, or about how to teach real lessons to real children. Hostility to achievement currently hides behind the word "equity" [meaning that] bright students must be tamped down so that slow learners will not feel bad about themselves. Grades and marks are bad, too because they distinguish and divide children. An actual curriculum, detailing things students ought to know, is viewed as cramping the human spirit. This lack of concern for achievement now has a racial cast. Asian and white children are often depicted as somehow out of step if they work harder and achieve more than blacks, Hispanics, and other minorities. Ed-school theory calls for strategies to conceal [the racial gap] under group

> projects or to demonstrate that achievement doesn't matter. (John Leo, *U.S. News*, 3 August 1998)

In June 2012, a study by the National Council on Teacher Quality in Washington, DC, indicated that California's teacher schools are among the worst in a nation full of substandard programs. They singled out UCLA and Loyola Marymount as prime offenders. Graduate teacher training programs in California are much more likely to accept lower achieving students and far less likely to provide feedback on such important skills as managing behavior in the classroom. The state's approach to training teachers focuses heavily on "addressing racist attitudes, gender bias, and classism." There is not enough instruction on subject matter and teaching methods.

California did require that all districts perform teacher evaluations based on how much the students have learned (as revealed in tests). So far (2015), only two small districts have complied (Teresa Watanable, *LA Times*, January 2015).

There is also an effort afoot to stop compensating teachers for graduate courses that are expensive to the school districts and do not improve the quality of teaching. In 2011, the Los Angeles Unified School

District spent 25 percent of its payroll compensating teachers for such course work. The new supervisor is pushing for these funds to be directed to those teachers who have proven results in the classroom, and achievement tests determine much of this. The union, of course, firmly opposes this.

Various experiments are also under way to let bright college graduates bypass education schools altogether. Connecticut has a program to allow graduates to switch into teaching from other careers by simply taking an eight-week summer course and passing a test. Teach for America also bypasses the education school swamp by picking the brightest students at prestige colleges and setting them loose in the classroom after just two weeks of preparation. But Teach for America's results have been mixed, and they have drawn the ire of teacher's unions.

MORE PAY FOR TEACHERS

It has long been proposed that higher pay will attract better teachers, and some have claimed this would narrow, if not close, the racial achievement gap. Linda Darling-Hammond, e.g., writes in the *Huffington Post* (20 August 2014) that teachers are only paid 60% of what other college graduates make, and that if their salaries were brought into line with those of other college grads, the achievement gap would decrease.

This is hard to reconcile with the decent performance of private school teachers who make around 30 percent less than their public school counterparts. It is also hard to reconcile with the experience of many American cities.

Chicago is and remains a troubled school district with dismal achievement test scores (and the usual racial gap). In 2012, the average pay of public school teachers stood at $75,000, among the highest in the nation. And they were offered another 16 percent pay raise conditional upon proven student achievement. This provoked a bitter strike that caught Mayor Rahm Emanuel and even President Obama off-guard, since they are close allies of the teacher's unions. In the end, they got their pay raise and the rule on effective teaching was gutted.

This pattern has been seen across the nation. Teachers, for a 9-month job, are handsomely paid in comparison with a few decades ago, and their retirement package is far better than what most in private industry can expect. In 1990, schools in Rochester, New York negotiated a contract that made the city's teachers the highest paid in the nation. It was hoped this would energize the efforts to reverse the dismal fortunes of the city's 33,000 students. But when the second 3 year term agreement was set to be signed with another hefty pay increase, the teachers narrowly defeated the contract since it contained a requirement for pay in the future to be tied to their performance. Many feared it would make them responsible for social conditions such as poverty and teenage pregnancy that greatly affect student performance and which are beyond their control.

There is some validity to this fear, but giving teachers additional thousands of dollars per year has done nothing to raise test scores (let alone to erase the gap). In Rochester in 2013, only 43% of students graduated and only 10% of those [i.e., 4.3% of the total] were ready for college.

Markham Middle School in Watts, Los Angeles is another example. Despite the best efforts of the many principals who have come and gone, and an army of well-intentioned reformers, private foundations, and corporate sponsors, the city attorney's office and—most recently—the mayor of Los Angeles, it continues to have one of the worst records of achievement in California.

The state spent thousands of dollars to develop an 11-point "research-based" plan for change, including teacher training and community involvement; this effort was scrapped as a failure in 1997. A second program in 1999 directed even more money into the school, boosting teacher salaries to well above the state average. This was also judged to be ineffective. And so it went year after year.

When Watts has the same things as Brentwood—a wealthy white neighborhood school—you might expect equal scores. But this has not been the case or the result.

Raising salaries has simply not worked. So can the teachers make a difference? In our final section, we will try to find some techniques that might work on a wider scale. More money neither raises test scores nor shrinks the achievement gap.

ABOLISHING TENURE

In the old days before unions hit the teacher ranks, it was assumed that a teacher deserved protection against changes in local government and public whims that might cost him his job. So after two to five years, teachers virtually everywhere were assured of their employment. Public school teachers are among the highest paid professionals in the nation, with an average salary of $76,000 per year including three month vacation time annually, full medical coverage and generous retirement funds they rarely pay into, which often supports them for many years in retirement. Because of union militancy, nothing can threaten the teacher; the huge war chests amassed by teachers' unions ensure that any serious candidate for political office finds it difficult to cross their wishes.

If a teacher is found to be ineffective, or even a sexual predator, it can take years to remove him or her-up to four years in California. Hearings have to be held, review upon review is needed.

But a movement has arisen to reduce the power of the teachers' union and reduce or eliminate tenure as unnecessary and even dangerous to students. Some have even claimed that the retention of poor teachers because of tenure is the explanation for the racial gap in achievement, since such teachers are more often found in heavily black and Hispanic schools.

In May 2012 lawyers representing nine public school students filed a lawsuit in California state court: *Vergara et al. v. California*. The suit alleged that California's tenure rules violated the California State Constitution by allowing grossly ineffective teachers to keep their jobs. This was alleged to have a disparate impact on poor and minority students, since they were more likely to be assigned to such teachers. In June, 2014 a Superior Court judge in Los Angeles ruled tenure unconstitutional since it denied an equal education to all students by permitting incompetent teachers to be retained based on years rather than performance. The judge's principal justification for the decision was the necessity of eliminating racial disparities in school and later life; bad teachers, he alleged, produce a lifetime deficit in earning among their pupils.

It is still too early to say for sure whether the abolition of tenure will close the racial achievement gap.

BETTER NEIGHBORHOODS

Liberals have long held that if poor kids could live in better neighborhoods and mix socially with wealthy kids, their scores would dramatically increase and the gap would close. This theory has now been tested in several ways, and the results are sobering.

1) The first big city to test the theory was Chicago, who moved 7,000 poor, mostly African American families into 100 virtually all-white neighborhoods across the Metropolitan area. This was in 1976. Initial studies promised important results. Not only had the tenants moved into more affluent and less crime-ridden neighborhoods, but their children indicated they were happy with their teachers, had better attitudes about school and were only a quarter as likely to drop out as children remaining in the unintegrated schools of the district. But there was no evidence to indicate test scores or IQ scores had increased for the children involved.

2) Nearly 20 years later, the US Department of Housing and Urban Development launched a highly expensive "Moving to Opportunity" program. Nearly 5,000 poor children in Boston, Baltimore, Los Angeles, New York, and Chicago were divided into three groups. An experimental group got vouchers and assistance in

moving to more affluent neighborhoods. A "treatment" group got housing vouchers for any private apartment or home, but no help moving into a neighborhood with less poverty. The control group stayed in public housing.

Four years later the researchers began checking the "experimental" and "treatment" groups to see if their performance had improved compared to children left behind in the projects. "The results of this very large-scale experiment indicate no evidence of improvement in reading scores, math scores, behavior problems or school engagement overall," the researchers report. Early results from one city, Baltimore, suggested that the program had a positive impact on children from kindergarten to sixth grade, but a long term analysis showed that the pupils did not sustain their gains. Overall, studies of the programs in all five cities showed "no appreciable educational or social improvement" ("Neighborhoods and Academic Achievement: Results from the Moving to Opportunity Experiment," National Bureau of Economic Research Working Paper No. 11909, by Lisa Sanbonmatsu, Jeffrey Kling, Greg Duncan, and Jeanne Brooks-Gunn).

3) The editors of *The Journal of Blacks in Higher Education* studied SAT scores of children of military families serving overseas, who attended 220 schools run by the army in 13 countries. They reasoned that military

schools enrolling black and white kids whose parents held similar jobs and earned similar incomes in a racially integrated culture would be ideal for testing whether the segregated neighborhoods of much of the United States are responsible for the large gap between the SAT scores of blacks and whites.

"No such luck," the magazine concluded. Black students of military personnel did score 38 SAT points higher than black students in public schools around the country, but as of 2005, the white students at Defense Department schools still scored 152 points higher than their black schoolmates on the combined SAT: 902 for blacks and 1054 for whites on a scale from 200 to 1600.

PRIVATE SCHOOLS

Long thought to be the bane of public schools, private schools have existed in this country since before its founding. During the battle over integration, thousands of white kids moved to private schools rather than attend class in distant black neighborhoods. In some districts, the percent could rise to 30 percent or more.

A study by the US Department of Education in 2006 determined that, while kids in private school seem to do better than those in public schools, when one takes into account their racial makeup, economic situation, and social condition, there was virtually no difference between public and private. In other words, private schools—with older buildings and with teachers who make half what public teachers make—break even with the achievement level of students in public schools. I think there is a lesson here.

VOUCHERS

A school voucher is a cash grant or tax credit given to parents for use toward the cost of educating their child at a school of their choice. School voucher programs have two principal aims: 1) to bring about greater racial integration (despite integration having been shown to have no educational effect), and 2) to introduce market style competition between school systems; it was hoped that even public schools would improve when forced to compete with private schools, just as the US Postal Service made improvement in its operation once faced with competition from private package carriers following deregulation in 1977.

Most vouchers are used by families in poor areas, who would otherwise have no choice but to send their children to the local public school. In many cities, a large percentage of those who were given vouchers went to parochial schools (80 percent in Milwaukee). Some observers believed this violated separation of church and state, but the Supreme Court (*Zelman v. Simmons-Harris*, 2002) decided 5–4 that vouchers did not violate the Constitution even when used for religious schools so long as the educational program had secular purposes.

The teachers' union opposed voucher programs, arguing that they would permit white students to move around as well, and thus reduce integration in many schools.

The advent of Charter Schools provided the final nail in the coffin of vouchers at a national level. Congress voted to abolish vouchers in all 50 states in 2002. Some states, however, such as Wisconsin, Indiana and Oklahoma, along with the District of Columbia, have continued with their own local version of vouchers for needy students at low achievement schools.

The Obamas opted out of the Washington, DC public schools and sent their children to Sidwell Friends, a first-rate private school with very high achievement records. But to the shock of many, President Obama removed from his 2016 budget funding for the school scholarship voucher program which allowed thousands of poverty ridden children to attend private and parochial schools of their choice. Why? Teacher union demands. The success of these private schools has given DC public education a black eye. Thus ended the final governmental vouchers program in the US.

Stephen Moore of the Heritage Foundation points out that if President Obama's budget passes, "schools like [Sidwell Friends] will be attended almost exclusively by kids of rich parents like the Obamas. Remember this the next time the president gives a lecture on income inequality and fairness." ("Leaving the Capitol's Children Behind," *Washington Times*, 8 February 2015)

CHARTER SCHOOLS

A "charter school" is a privately managed school funded by taxes. The first charters were set up by motivated parents; more recently, private companies have been founded to run them. If a charter school succeeds in raising student achievement, it is allowed to continue; if it fails, it is supposed to be closed. In 1991, Minnesota passed the first law enabling the creation of charter schools free to students but operated independently from the local school district. Since then, 5,000 such schools have opened in 39 states.

In 2009, Stanford University's Center for Research on Educational Outcomes issued a long report on charter schools. The schools studied range from Nevada, which has no oversight over such schools, to California, which has excessive oversight through state regulations and local district rules. The report found that charter schools are twice more likely to do worse by their students than regular schools; only 17 percent of charters provide education superior to that of traditional public schools. In Nevada, charter school students are thought to have lost the equivalent of half a year's schooling. They called the charter movement a failed experiment in privatization.

Researchers also found that academics is far down the list of reasons parents send their children to charters. Local convenience and the sense that parents get more respect are the primary reasons.

Half of charter schools that should be shut down aren't, due to the political connections of the private companies running the schools or to wealthy donors or parent groups who simply demand they stay open.

In Los Angeles Unified School District (LAUSD), on the other hand, two charter schools run by Aspire, one of the top private charter school firms, were closed in spite of performing well. This was because Aspire contracted with a company outside the LAUSD to provide special education programs for handicapped children! The school board decided, effective 2013, that any charter using services other than those of the district would be closed. The Average Performance Index at the two Aspire-run schools had risen to 800, which is the declared statewide goal. Aspire had achieved this with a school body of which 90 percent qualified for subsidized lunches and most were not fluent in English. Obviously, academic success is not the only criterion by which charter schools are judged.

MAGNET SCHOOLS

Magnet schools are public schools with specialized courses or curricula which can draw students from across more than one geographically defined school district. The original idea was to achieve racial integration without resorting to forced busing. The first magnet school of which I have found record was the Los Angeles Center for Enriched Studies, established in 1977 as part of Los Angeles' effort to replace mandatory busing with a voluntary integration plan. In 1997 it won the legal right to discriminate based on race in a court ruling that said magnet schools were outside the scope of Proposition 209, passed in 1996, which forbade consideration of race in school and college admissions. So this school is strictly limited as to how many of each racial group is allowed in.

A story in the *Los Angeles Times* (13 December 2007) states that "the school is successful among all races, although there remains a significant gap between Asian and white students and their African-American and Hispanic counterparts. White students, for instance, had an API score of 893 in this year while Hispanics lagged at 774 and African Americans at 733, still well ahead of district and state averages."

The reports gathered in 2014 for the previous five years shows that they have dropped a few points, but the racial differences remain despite all efforts. It is obvious that even carefully orchestrated racial integration and careful selection of students do not close the achievement gap.

ACADEMIES

An "academy," as the term is currently used by school reformers, is a mini-school set up within a larger public school. Several academies may be contained within a single school, with the aim of grouping pupils with those of similar ability and giving them the sense of belonging to a smaller community. Kids are assigned to one academy and normally remain in it for the duration of their school time.

Since its inception in 1967, Locke High School in Watts had been a troubled institution, with dismal graduation rates, graffiti-covered walls, fights frequently breaking out, and students wandering the halls during class time. Unionized teachers urged that the school be reopened under a charter. In 2008, a private company called Green Dot took over. The student body at that time was 40% black and 60% Hispanic.

Among the first changes introduced by Green Dot was to assign all incoming 9th graders to one of four newly created academies. One was geared toward preparing students for college; another was for students Green Dot considered would be better served by learning a trade or skill. In addition, students in the other grades were to be put into several academies where they too would stay with the same teachers during their remaining school years at Locke.

Green Dot also hired many bright new teachers from "Teach for America." Each had volunteered for the opportunity to make a difference in this, the most troubled school in Los Angeles. The school began to attract visitors such as Los Angeles Mayor Villaraigosa, Secretary of Education Arne Duncan, California's Superintendent of Education, two US Senators and three Congressmen.

Then things began to unravel. Thirty percent of the teachers resigned after the first year, 30% more after the 2nd year; the Dean quit, and two principals were fired. The main reason teachers cited for leaving was "unsafe conditions." Some teachers were threatened by students, some spat upon, some beaten and all subject to a constant drone of foul language and other disrespectful behavior. It didn't help that the government ordered discipline relaxed at this very time. The students took full advantage. One put a teacher in the hospital but returned after a single day's suspension; he was back in school before the teacher was able to leave the hospital.

Soon it became evident that achievement test scores and graduation rates were actually dropping. Despite extra remedial education and special tutors, the percentage of ninth graders testing "below basic" or "far below basic" in math increased sharply. One of the academies, Animo Locke Technology Academy, was rated 1382nd out of 1444 schools. Of the Locke students who did go onto college, only two percent did not require remedial classes. Clearly, "academies" had failed to improve the test scores of the school's black and Hispanic student body, and thus were making no progress toward closing the racial gap. When the final principal quit in 2013, the program was terminated and Locke High School was closed forever.

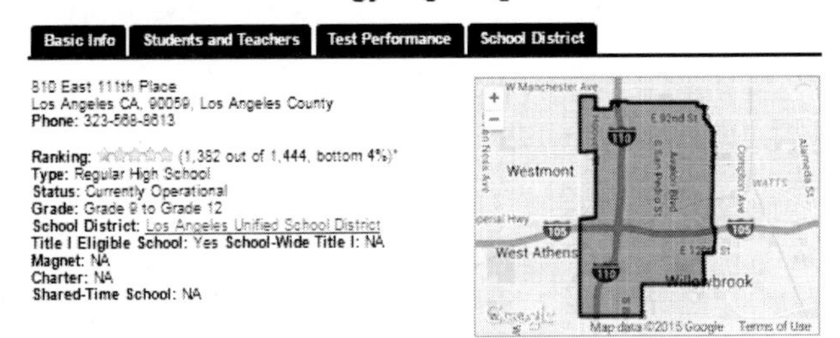

Students and Teachers

	2012-2013		2011-2012		2010-2011		2009-2010		2008-2009		2007-2008	
	Amount	%	Amount	%	Amount	%	Amount	%	Amount	%	Amount	%
Total Teachers:	25		23		NA	NA	18		14		9	
Total Students:	462		539		547		410		289		124	
Grade 9:	110	23.8%	145	26.9%	NA	NA	122	29.8%	154	53.3%	124	100.0%
Grade 10:	126	27.3%	138	25.6%	NA	NA	158	38.5%	135	46.7%	0	0.0%
Grade 11:	114	24.7%	132	24.5%	NA	NA	130	31.7%	0	0.0%	0	0.0%
Grade 12:	112	24.2%	124	23.0%	NA	NA	0	0.0%	0	0.0%	0	0.0%
Ungraded:	NA	NA	NA	NA	NA	NA	NA	NA	NA	NA	NA	NA
Student By Gender:												
Male:	235	50.9%	277	51.4%	NA	NA	204	49.8%	148	51.2%	59	47.6%
Female:	227	49.1%	262	48.6%	NA	NA	206	50.2%	141	48.8%	61	49.2%
Student By Races:												
American Indian/Alaska Native:	0	0.0%	1	0.2%	NA	NA	0	0.0%	0	0.0%	0	0.0%
Asian:	0	0.0%	0	0.0%	NA	NA	0	0.0%	0	0.0%	11	8.9%
Hispanic:	350	75.8%	371	68.8%	NA	NA	296	72.2%	197	68.2%	75	60.5%
Black:	109	23.6%	163	30.2%	NA	NA	114	27.8%	85	29.4%	38	30.6%
White:	0	0.0%	0	0.0%	NA	NA	0	0.0%	0	0.0%	0	0.0%
Hawaiian Native/Pacific Islander:	0	0.0%	0	0.0%	NA	NA	0	0.0%	6	2.1%	NA	NA
Two or More Races:	3	0.6%	4	0.7%	NA	NA	0	0.0%	1	0.3%	NA	NA
Lunch Program:												
Free Lunch Program Eligible:	407	88.1%	NA	NA	NA	NA	373	91.0%	240	83.0%	101	81.5%
Reduced-Price Lunch Program Eligible:	28	6.1%	NA	NA	NA	NA	14	3.4%	19	6.6%	9	7.3%
Student-Teacher Ratio:	18.19		23.85		NA	NA	22.78		19.30		13.80	

Test Performance

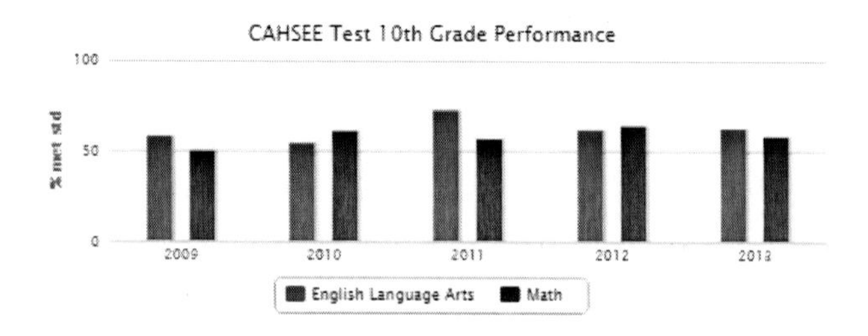

California Academic Performance Index (API) Score

The academic Performance Index (API) is a single number assigned to each school by the California Department of Education to measure overall school performance and improvement over time on statewide testing. The API ranges from 2000 to 1000, with 800 or higher as the state goal for all schools.

Index ix

The public schools of Inglewood, California (85 percent black) made similar efforts with similar results. Only 25 percent of its students are at grade level in English and four percent in math. Enrollments are in free fall as students transfer to other school districts or go to charter schools. The school district is in bankruptcy. The following charts relate to one of these Inglewood Schools

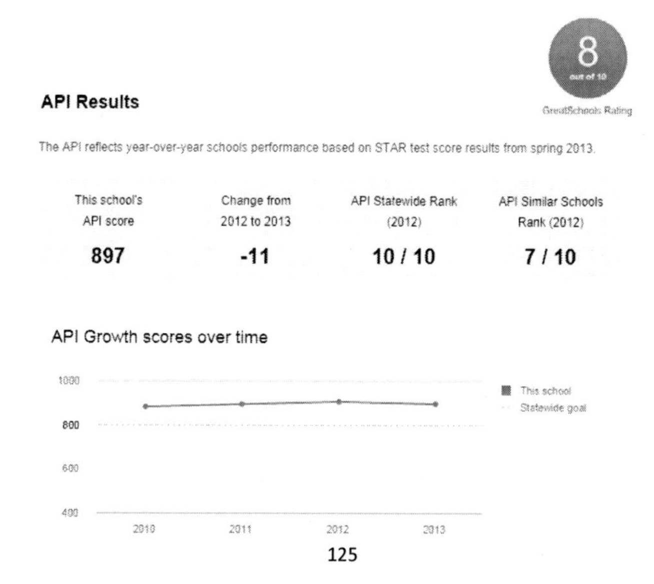

API Growth scores by subgroup

In addition to schoolwide API scores, each student subgroup receives an API score.

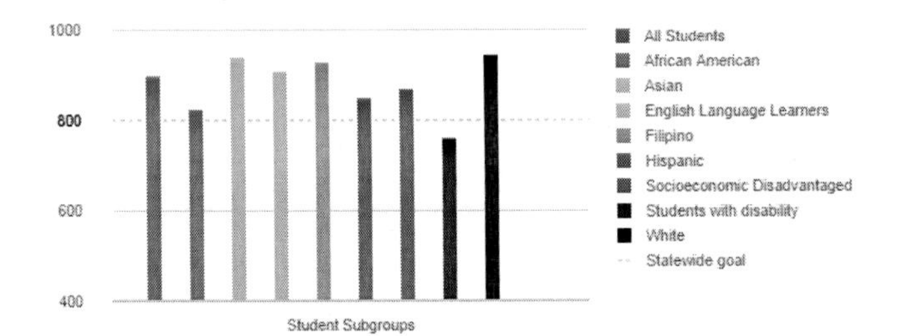

This school's API score

897

What is the API?

The Academic Performance Index (API) is a single number assigned to each school by the California Department of Education to measure overall school performance and improvement over time on statewide testing. The API ranges from 200 and 1000, with 800 as the state goal for all schools.

Change from 2012 to 2013

-11

Change from 2012 to 2013

Comparing the API Growth to the Base shows whether or not this school's test score performance improved between Spring 2012 and Spring 2013. The API ranges between 200 and 1000, with 800 as the statewide goal for all schools. Schools scoring below an 800 are given at least a 5 point target for the next year.

API Statewide Rank (2012)

10 / 10

API Statewide Rank (2012)

The API Statewide Rank ranges from 1 to 10. A rank of 10, for example, means that the school's API fell into the top 10% of all schools in the state with a comparable grade range. The 2012 rank is based on results from tests students took in Spring 2012.

API Similar Schools Rank (2012)

7 / 10

API Similar Schools Rank (2012)

The API Similar Schools Rank ranges from 1 to 10. It shows how the school compares to other schools with similar student demographic profiles. The California Department of Education uses parent education level, poverty level, student ethnicity and other data to identify similar schools.

Index x

PAYING STUDENTS TO DO BETTER IN SCHOOL

This controversial approach involves giving kids cash proportionate to their attendance, grades, and the number of books they have read. Many have called it bribery.

Edward Deci, a prominent psychologist from the University of Rochester, has spent years studying motivation. He doubts payment will help any kids over the long term. He points to a study done in 1977 which showed that rewards can have the perverse effect of making people perform worse. This study was done in a nursery school by Stanford University with toddlers being rewarded for drawing. The same classroom included a control group of children not offered any reward. After the rewards had been given out, observation through a one-way mirror showed that the kids who got the rewards only did half-hearted art work in the ensuing days, while the others seem to enjoy drawing for its own sake.

Nonetheless, a program of paying children to do well in school was launched in a number of school districts. The focus was primarily on blacks and Hispanics, mostly in the poorer areas of town. The money came primarily from charitable groups and wealthy donors. The kids seemed happy to get the money, and the districts were hopeful it could mark a turnaround. But the results have been mixed at best.

In New York City, beginning in 2007, $1.5 million was paid to 8,320 kids for good grades. This was done as part of the mayor's anti-poverty program, which also paid $50 per month to parents for their child's attendance and an additional $25 for attending parent-teacher conferences. Overall this pay program cost the city about $53 million by 2010 and had no lasting effect on any level.

In Chicago, with a different model, the kids who earned money for grades attended class more often and did get better grades, but did not do better on their standardized tests.

In Houston, a privately funded $1.5 million program was implemented in 2010 to reward 5th graders when they master basic math standards. Each family could earn up to $1,050. The program was terminated when it became apparent that test scores and achievement rankings were not improving.

In Louisville, the Kentucky Educational Excellence Scholarship provides up to $500 in state lottery funds to kids with all A's. According to teacher Chris

Spoonamore, parents "rip teachers" when their child is given a C.

Results in Washington, DC were more promising. Kids got paid for attendance and behavior, and that seemed to lead to more learning effort. They did better on standardized reading tests.

But the example of Dallas warns us to beware of short-term gains. The Dallas school district paid second graders to read books, and this improved their scores on standardized tests at the end of the year. They even continued to do better the next year, after the rewards had stopped. But by the sixth grade, the advantage dried up, and their tests scores averaged the same as those not part of the experiment. This pattern is similar to what was observed with Head Start.

Dallas also tried paying students $400 to take and pass Advanced Placement tests. The only effect was that large numbers of unqualified students attempted the tests.

COMBATING TEST APPREHENSION IN MINORITY PUPILS

With increased attention to test scores as the most important criterion of student performance, student anxiety about taking tests may also be rising. "Schools and teachers are under a lot of pressure to meet standards and the pressure gets passed onto the students," says Nathaniel von der Embse, a psychologist at East Carolina University. "The prevalence of test anxiety has certainly risen along with the use of test-based accountability." What's worse, he says, is that test anxiety can expand over time into any situation in which the student is conscious of being evaluated—from a class presentation to a college admission exam such as the SAT. And, it is feared, it can lead to diminished self-esteem, reduced motivation, and disengagement from school.

Some argue that the failure of minorities to do well in achievement tests should be attributed to test apprehension. Such a theory requires us to assume that minority children feel *greater* anxiety when taking tests than do white or Asian children. Champions of the test apprehension theory argue, accordingly, that blacks and Hispanics face an anxiety specific to their groups about "fitting a stereotype of failure." In a paper submitted in

1995 in the Journal of Personality and Social Psychology, Claude Steel of Stanford and Joshua Aronson of the University of Texas argue that pervasive negative stereotypes about blacks' intellectual ability creates a "situational pressure" that distracts them and depresses their academic performance.

There are steps young people can take which are said to calm them down and reduce negative thoughts before a test. There is even said to be a "values-affirmation exercise" that shrinks the performance gap between black and white students by 40 percent, and erases the gender gap altogether. But it is difficult to measure "test anxiety" precisely and, therefore, to know whether such exercises work. And even if they do, they are likely to help white and Asian children as much as blacks and Hispanics, leaving no net effect on the racial gap.

It is known that white and Asian parents tend to place greater stress on academic achievement, and that whites and Asians score higher on the personality trait psychologists call "conscientiousness" than is the case with black and Hispanic children. Both these facts would lead us to expect white and Asian children to experience greater anxiety when taking tests or otherwise being evaluated. Steel and Aronson's "situational pressure" specific to blacks, on the other hand, is pure speculation.

HORSE SENSE

Dennis Parker is a horseman and former teacher who lives on a small ranch outside Sacramento. He has been hired by a number of districts at a salary of thousands of dollars per day to teach teachers how to boost achievement and test results in academically poor schools. His basic philosophy of maintaining a "good relationship" with students is based on the methods he uses to train horses. He claimed in 2012 that his advice and direction have had a dramatic impact on test scores at Wilson Elementary School in Santa Ana and Artesia High School in Lakewood.

A closer look at these two schools indicates the opposite. While some improvement is noted at Wilson, the test scores have never reached the district average, which itself is well below the state average. In 2013, Wilson Elementary ranked worse than 71.8 percent of the elementary schools in California and 21st out of 37 schools in Santa Ana. At Artesia High School, the goal set for the Academic Performance Index (API) is a modest 800 on a scale of 200–1000. In 2013, a score of 777 was 11 points lower than the previous year. It does match other schools of similar ethnic composition (68 percent Hispanic).

KEEPING LOUSE-INFESTED STUDENTS IN CLASS

Perhaps the strangest proposal inspired by the desire to protect students' self-esteem is keeping children infected with head lice in class. This policy is said to be aimed at avoiding embarrassment to children and protecting their privacy, as well as to keep them from missing instruction. We suspect the real motives have more to do with keeping the flow of tax dollars coming into the districts. One district in Nevada airily advised parents not to worry, but to check their kid's hair once a week for infestation.

Parents are understandably concerned about this unhygienic practice, and incidences of lice are increasing. The Centers for Disease Control and Prevention says there are now 6–12 million cases per year involving children 3 to 11 years old.

No figures are available yet on whether lousy students are achieving more than they would if properly disinfected.

HISPANIC SERVING INSTITUTIONS

This is a brand new category of costly efforts to close the achievement gap. For years the UC Santa Barbara was perceived as a white college campus where Latinos felt "out of place." But last year, 2014, Latinos increased to over 25% of the student body, officially qualifying the school as a "Hispanic Serving Institution," earning it membership in the Hispanic Association of Colleges and Universities.

This status is the first step toward enabling such schools to receive federal and private grants aimed at bolstering the academic success of Latinos. How this can be done without violating the State's ban on affirmative action remains to be seen. The new status is shared by 261 other schools around the nation, including 91 in California. It remains to be seen if these additional funds and government programs have any impact on achievement tests or do anything but increase the welfare assistance they are afforded (and which is denied to Asians, whites and blacks).

RESEGREGATING STUDENTS

Surely the most ironic suggestion for eliminating the racial gap is reintroducing some form of racial segregation. In Topeka, Kansas, subject of the original *Brown* decision, retiring school superintendent Robert McFrazier remarked on the occasion of the fiftieth anniversary of *Brown* that the decision was a social triumph but an educational failure. He thinks integration has been given a fair chance, and that all schools now have the adequate equipment some lacked in the past. Black students now have access to newer books and better facilities in common with their white peers, but as a group they still perform well below white students. On a statewide Kansas reading test, 34 percent of black kids scored unsatisfactorily compared to just 13 percent of whites. Why? Ironically, McFrazier blames the end of segregation. He argues that closing black neighborhood schools—with their traditions, yearbooks, mottoes, fight songs, and halls of fame—uprooted these communities. While he believes the original court decision was justified, he thinks 50 years have shown that desegregation and better schools do not help black students academically, and that a new course must be found.

With one in four young black men either in jail or on probation, few attending college and many of those dropping out, a vocal minority of black educators are advocating separate classrooms for elementary school age black boys. Advocates believe that low expectations, absence of positive role models, and low self-esteem are largely responsible for the failure of African American boys to achieve in school, and that these problems could be mitigated by all-black classrooms. In 1987, an effort of this sort was made in Dade County, Florida. Two such classrooms were set up and run for a year. The experiment seemed to produce good results: absentee rates dropped six percent, and test scores jumped six percent. Additionally, there was a noticeable decrease in hostile behavior. But the US Education Department closed it down as a violation of civil rights law. The only similar program remaining is in Washington, DC, a private endeavor run by a group called Concerned Black Men. Detractors say that separating students by race or sex could intensify black boys' feelings of anger and inferiority.

NO CHILD LEFT BEHIND

The No Child Left Behind Act (NCLB) was a reauthorization, with amendments, of the Elementary and Secondary Education Act of 1965, the major federal law authorizing federal spending on K-12 schooling. Its full title was "An act to close the achievement gap with accountability, flexibility, and choice, so that no child is left behind." Proposed by incoming President George W. Bush in 2001, the act was approved by both houses of congress with bipartisan support, and was signed into law in January 2002. NCLB required states to establish standards for students at all grade levels, with the goal of having all students at proficiency level within twelve years (i.e., by 2014). States were also required to test students periodically to assess progress toward the goal of universal proficiency, and to report the results in the aggregate and for specific student subgroups, including low-income students, students with disabilities, English language learners and major racial and ethnic groups. The bill provided for large increases in federal funding for all school districts that complied with its requirements.

NCLB provided for penalties for schools unable to keep up with the goals of the program. After two years, students were allowed to transfer to a school with a better record. After three years, schools were required to provide tutoring and other help for struggling students on an individual basis. After five years, a "restructuring plan" would be drawn up; this might involve converting the school to a charter, firing all the teachers, or closing the school altogether. If the school was still below standard after six years, the restructuring plan would be implemented.

What have been the results from all this investment in the past 15 years? In fourth grade reading, the gains after implementation of NCLB (No Child Left Behind), were a mere three points. In 8th grade reading there were no gains. (Report by John Ghubb, *Education Next, 2009, vol 9,no 3)*

Over half of poor and minority children have reading and math skills far below grade level, whether measured by the tough performance standards of the NAEP (National Assessment of Education Progress) or by the (often weaker) standards of the various states. Dropout rates have been measured accurately only since NCLB required such record keeping as part of Title 1 funding: they hover around 50% in many major cities.

School choice and tutoring have proven to be ineffective. Fewer than five percent of eligible students chose to leave their "failing" school. Kids hate to leave their neighborhood, friends, and social life, and in some depressed areas there may not be an approved school within several miles. Only about 15% of students eligible for tutoring actually signed up, and evaluations from a number of states show that tutored students did no better on state tests than their untutored peers. Legislators had assumed that students in poor schools would jump at the chance to transfer to better schools or receive special tutoring, but both assumptions proved unwarranted.

In 2006, 29 percent of schools were failing to make adequate yearly progress; by 2010, the figure had risen to 38 percent. Fear of losing their jobs or missing bonuses lead many administrators to misreport test results. The nation's biggest cheating scandal involved 44 schools and 180 educators in Atlanta. Eleven persons were convicted on racketeering charges and sentenced to prison terms of up to 7 years.

In 2011, US Secretary of Education Arne Duncan, issued warnings that 82% of schools would be labeled as "failing" that year. The numbers didn't turn out quite that high, but several states did see failure rates over 50% (McNeil, *Education Week*, 3 August 2011)

The reason for Duncan's scare tactics was that the Department of Education had already seized upon a new sure-fire method for closing the achievement gap and achieving unprecendented educational progress: Common Core. Duncan allowed states to opt out of the failing NCLB program and convert to Common Core if they met certain criteria and adopted some of the Obama administration's educational priorities. Thirty-two states and the District of Columbia did so.

By 2014, when NCLB was supposed to have achieved its aims, it had already been forgotten.

COMMON CORE

The latest fad is known as "common core." Its roots stretch back to the so-called standards and accountability movement of the 1990s. At that time, a number of US states began establishing statewide standards for what students were expected to know and to be able to do at each grade level, as well as methods for assessing whether students were meeting the standards. Gradually, a movement coalesced to extend this approach to the entire United States.

In June, 2009 the National Governors Association and the Council of Chief State School Officers published their first set of nationwide standards for English and Math, as part of what they call the Common Core State Standards Initiative. These standards are supposed to embody what colleges and employers expect of high school graduates. They cover every grade from kindergarten through twelfth, and will eventually be expanded to include all academic subjects.

The details were developed by a group called Achieve, funded to the tune of $713 million by the Gates Foundation. Federal laws prohibit the US Department of Education from prescribing any curriculum, but $4 billion in initial funding for the states adopting it is a big carrot. There was no input from teachers or parents or local school districts.

David Feith writes in the *Wall Street Journal, June 2013,* that:

> Common Core is about an obsession with race, class, gender, and sexuality as the forces of history and political identity . . . Nationalizing education via Common Core is about promoting an agenda of anti-capitalism, sustainability, white guilt, global citizenship, self-esteem, effective math and culture sensitive spelling and language. All this is done in the name of consciousness raising, moral relativity, fairness, diversity, and multiculturalism.

Common Core encourages "educational gaming," meaning that students play supposedly educational games on their computers. Classics from the past such as *Huckleberry Finn* have been removed from approved reading lists.

One member of the Common Core Validation Committee, Stanford professor Dr. James Milgram, refused to sign off on the mathematics portion. "The Core Mathematics Standards are written to reflect very low expectations," he said, calling them "as non-challenging as possible."

Yet, at the same time, students are not given the ordinary tools they need to do simple math. Since Common Core advocates claim that "memorization is worthless," students do not memorize the multiplication table. Instead, they are loaded down with a great number of mathematical formulas, for which they develop cheat sheets. Eight year olds need calculators to get their homework done, ending up calculator cripples.

Any student who marks an incorrect answer on one of the Common Core assessment tests is given an alternative question instead, to help bolster the results. Children are even allowed to opt out from the annual tests. The California Privacy Protection Plan allows any parent to have their kids excused from any tests during the year and at the end of their class year. How will the public be able to tell how the program is doing?

And the entire program has been copyrighted, so that no changes can be made without their express permission.
At first, Common Core was greeted with wild enthusiasm; forty-four states and the District of Columbia signed up for it. Kentucky and New York were the first to implement it, in 2011 and 2012, even

before the proper text books were published or teachers were trained in accordance with the new curriculum.

While the class curriculum has been dumbed down, the tests themselves has been made more difficult.. In Kentucky, when the first results came in, only half of elementary students were found to be proficient or better in reading—compared to three quarters the year before under the old program.

New York found that only 30 percent of their students could pass the tests, and the achievement gap between the races grew slightly. In one Harlem school, only seven percent received passing scores in English, and ten percent in math. Businessman George Ball put it this way: "We have gone from No Child Left Behind to Just About Every Child Left Behind—if helplessness is the Common Core's goal, it's a stunning success."(*Time* magazine, June 2014)

In one district, 60 percent of the students declined even to take the test as a form of protest against the Common Core agenda. Teacher pay is tied to school tests in New York, so teachers often lack enthusiasm for the curriculum as well. Some observers ascribe the poor results to trying to do too much, too fast.

When some New York parents protested at what they saw, the US Education Secretary dismissed the outcry as coming from "white suburban moms who—all of a sudden—realize their child is not as bright as they thought." This did little to win supporters for this new program.

Other areas of the country are getting the message. An *LA Times* editorial (24 March 2014) warned schools against rushing into Common Core. The editorial encourages the Obama administration to consider that Common Core still has flaws that need to be worked out before this program spreads nationally. Second, the schools should be given a few years to implement and work with the program before teachers are evaluated by the results. Third, implementation should not begin until textbooks and teachers are ready for a new program.

For Santa Ana schools, the results of implementing Common Core were disastrous. The school district, however, put on a brave face, announcing to the world that serious progress had been made at two of its schools. It turns out that these particular schools are over 70% white and 10% Asian in a district that is 92% Hispanic overall. See Appendix 10 for details.

Liberals are concerned about teacher evaluations based on Common Core results and conservatives are worried the program is a further encroachment by the national government into what have always been local school decisions. Traditional standardized achievement tests such as the SAT and ACT are being phased out in favor of Common Core, which may make the program's success harder to measure.

Initial results have already thrown fear and disarray into the new program. Some states have already withdrawn their support, while others have lowered the standards that define "success." Supporters continue to hope and promise that Common Core will help close the achievement gap between the ethnic groups, but nothing in the early results would lead one to believe this.

DECLINING STANDARDS

The effort to eliminate achievement differentials between the races has been accompanied by a significant decline in overall academic standards. Already in 1983, *A Nation at Risk*, the report by President Reagan's National Commission on Excellence in Education, warned that declining standardized test scores were largely the result of an erosion of academic standards in the nation's high schools. That erosion, the study says, is reflected in rampant grade inflation, increased absenteeism, easier textbooks, large increases in the number of elective courses allowed, and a decreased emphasis on reading and writing, along with a general tendency to demand less of students than formerly.[10] Grade inflation serves to mask the decline. As Thomas Sowell reports: "American high schools gave out approximately twice as many C's as A's in 1966 but by 1978, the A's exceeded the C's. By 1986, more than one-fifth of all entering freshmen in college averaged A– or above for their entire high school careers."[11]

The educational establishment is afraid to enforce standards because of the effect it would have on the lives

---

[10] Don Speich, *Los Angeles Times*, January 17, 1987.

[11] Thomas Sowell, *Education: Assumptions vs. History* (Hoover Institution Press, 1986).

of students unable to meet them. In 1999, the Massachusetts State Board of Education set a low passing mark on its new statewide graduation exam so as not to drive weak pupils to drop out or put them at a disadvantage in trying to get a job later. Wisconsin scrapped their plans for graduation exams altogether after protests from parents. (*US News*, 13 December 1999)

The state of Georgia bragged that 85% of its students met or exceeded the proficiency benchmark on its 2007 tests. But only 28% of the same students scored high enough to be considered proficient on the National Assessment of Educational Progress or NAEP, administered by the US Department of Education. Georgia, like many states, sets its proficiency standards so low that barely literate students can be deemed proficient. Alarmingly, five other states have even lower standards. Fifteen states lowered their levels between 2009 and 2011. Since 2012, New York students can pass the English exam required for high school graduation with a grade of 55 out of 100.

In view of the dismal results obtained in graduation and achievement exams in Los Angeles, rigorous graduation requirements set in 2005 were dramatically reduced five years later. Students can now pass college preparation courses with only a D grade, even though California colleges require a C average for admission. The California state legislature also passed a law exempting most students with disabilities from taking the test. The number of units needed to graduate was also reduced so that more students could graduate. "I know of no other school district which is reducing graduation requirements by 60 units could then call such action an improvement [*sic*]," said former senior district official, Sharon Robinson. The school district called the changes a "creative solution." Scores are expected to drop farther once California adopts Common Core in the Fall of 2015.

The College Board, which administers the SAT test, made an effort to raise standards in 2006 with a new, longer version of the test. The result was the largest drop in scores in three decades. The racial gap, which had already increased by 5.5 percent between 1975 and 2005, grew even larger by another 7% with the new version of the test (which had supposedly been freed of cultural bias). Rather than address the problems directly, a campaign was mounted to have college admissions departments disregard the SAT test, and many are doing so. But with grades meaning ever less due to grade inflation and dumbed-down curricula, the elimination of the SAT will leave little for admissions officers to look at. College Board Chairman, David Coleman announced (5 March 2014) that the SAT would be revised again in

2016. This was needed, he said, because the test had become "far too disconnected from the work in our high schools." The real reason may have more to do with averting a general abandonment of the SAT.

The 2013 testing done by the National Assessment of Educational Progress, measured 92,000 high school seniors in the United States and found that reading scores are lower than those of students in 1992. Seventy-four percent of students score below the grade-appropriate level in math. At the same time, graduation rates have climbed to an all-time high.

Some of this decline can be attributed to shifting demographics. The achievement gap between white and black/Hispanic students remains very wide, while the percent of white twelfth graders has fallen from 74 percent in 1992 to 58 percent in 2013.

The United States has slid to 29th in the world for math ability in 2012, down from 23rd just three years earlier. In science, we lag behind 22 nations, falling from 18th in 2009. In reading, the United States was behind 19 countries, falling from 9th in 2009. How can America maintain its prosperity and strength in the face of these trends?

Pentagon data (12 December 2010) shows that 75 percent of 17–24 year olds don't qualify for the military because they are physically unfit, have a criminal record, or didn't graduate from high school. Of those who do graduate from high school, 23 percent don't get the minimum score needed to enlist in any branch of the military. (The Education Trust, 21 December 2010)

Even civilian employers are finding it difficult to fill skilled positions, despite all the money poured into American schools. "The so-called skills gap is now threatening to impede economic growth…with more than half of the companies in a new survey saying they have struggled to recruit candidates for open positions, especially at the higher end of the wage spectrum…And the recruitment problem includes skilled trade jobs as well." (Tiffany Hsu, *LA Times*, 31 October 2014)

By 2020, the United States is expected to face a shortage of 1.5 million workers with degrees, and 6 million people who lack even a high school diploma (*US News*, January 2014.*)*

Concurrent with eroding standards is a tendency to infantilize college students. Professors at UC Santa Barbara, for example, are required to mention in their course descriptions anything that might be upsetting to students taking their classes. Such students can then be excused from those classes without penalty. A student might claim, for instance, that taking remedial English would make him feel like a failure; another might be upset by the views of a professor perceived as too conservative, too religious, or too anything else.

Oberlin College in Ohio has gone further. Professors have to avoid any topic that might cause trauma due to racism, sexism, heterosexism, gender identity issues, "ableism" (discrimination against the disabled) and other issues of privilege and oppression.

The following chart illustrates the level of income to be obtained by entering one of the trades without college and the growth anticipated in the future along side some that do require college.

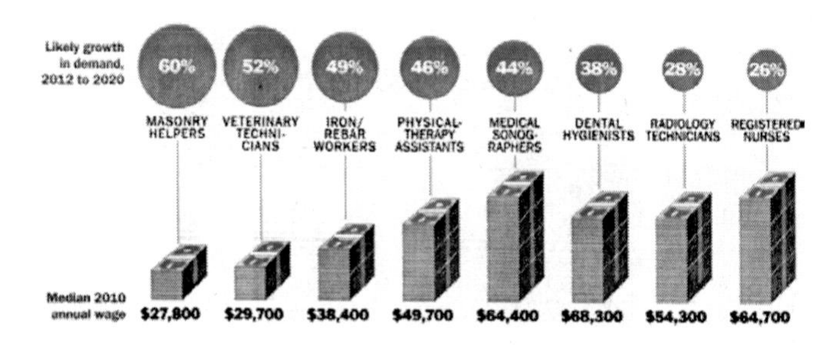

Index xi

THE DISCIPLINE GAP

When I was young in the 1950s and 1960s, leading school discipline issues included the throwing of spitballs and talking out of turn. Since integration in the 1960s, however, American schools have witnessed a dramatic increase in serious criminal violence. Between 1970 and 1973, school-related homicides increased by 18 percent. Rapes went up by 40 percent, robberies by 37 percent, assaults on teachers by 77 percent, and drug offenses by 38 percent (*US News*, 26 January 1976). By March 1980, a noted Los Angeles psychiatrist who had treated more than 200 teachers stated: "The combination of continued violence and threats of violence with little or no support from school administrators results in teachers who experience psychological and physiological depletion and ultimately collapse under the stress." This is particularly common in the poorer areas of Los Angeles; it is called "battered teacher syndrome," displaying similarities to World War I shell shock or combat fatigue. Turnover among teachers in many public school districts is high, and violent and unruly pupils are the main reason teachers cited. (Institute of Educational Sciences, "Teacher" article by Robert Paulker, vs. 97, page 46-77, March 1980)

Here are some more recent figures:

In 2012, 749,000 nonfatal violent victimizations were reported at US schools among students 12-18 years old. Nine percent of teachers report that they have been threatened with injury by a student from their school; five percent say they have actually been attacked (the highest percentage ever).

A 2013 poll of youth in grades 9-12 taken by the Center for Disease Control and Prevention found the following:

> 8.1% reported being in a physical fight on school property in the 12 months prior to the survey.
>
> 7.1% reported that they did not go to school on one or more days in the 30 days prior to the survey because they felt unsafe at or on the way to school.
>
> 5.2% reported carrying a weapon on school property on one or more days in the 30 days prior to the survey.
>
> 6.9% reported being threatened or injured with a weapon on school property one or more times in the 12 months prior to the survey.

> 19.6% reported being bullied on school property and 14.8% reported being "electronic bullied" during the 12 months prior to the survey.

Bullying has become a national problem, and awareness of it is increasing. Unfortunately, much of the discussion is distorted by politically correct thinking, with an over-emphasis on occasional instances in which homosexuals or racial minorities are the victims. Most bullying does not fit this pattern, however.

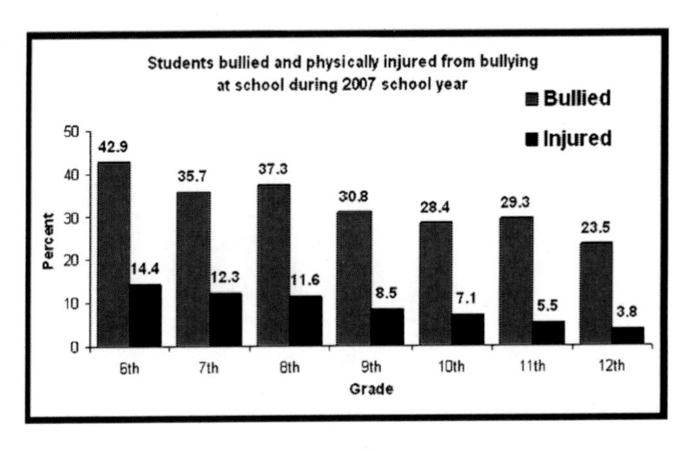

Index xii

DID YOU KNOW...

- **More than 160,000 U.S. students stay home from school each day from fear of being bullied**
- **8% of students miss 1 day of class per month for fear of Bullies**
- **Playground statistics - Every 7 minutes a child is bullied**
- **77% of students are bullied mentally, verbally, & physically**
- **Bullying is the most common form of violence. Between 15 percent and 30 percent of students are bullies or victims**
- **Direct, physical bullying increases in elementary school, peaks in middle school, and declines in high school verbal abuse, on the other hand, remains constant**
- **43% fear harassment in the bathroom at school**
- **282,000 students are physically attacked in secondary schools each month**
- **1 out of 5 kids admits to being a bully, or doing some "Bullying"**
- **22% of Student know someone who has been bullied online**
- **19% of students admit to saying something hurtful to others online**
- **Over 14 percent of high school students have considered suicide, and almost 7 percent have attempted it**
- **About 35 percent of kids have been threatened online**
- **A poll of teens ages 12-17 proved that they think violence increased at their schools**

Index xiii

The races do not contribute equally to school discipline problems. The US Department of Health and Human Services (HHS) reported that in the 1972–1973 school-year, more than three times as many black students as whites suffered suspension.

In Connecticut in 2002, 52 percent of all suspensions in elementary schools involved black students, who made up only 13 percent of the school population; in other words, they were over-represented by a factor of four. During the same year, Hispanics constituted 18 percent of elementary school pupils and received 35 percent of suspensions—over-representation by a factor slightly less than two. The white majority accounted for only 12 percent of suspensions. During the 2011-12 school year, 998 students under the age of seven were suspended in Connecticut, and more than three quarters of these very young children were black or Hispanic. (Linda Conner Lambreck in CTPOST.com 2013)

In Los Angeles, black students account for about 11 percent of the student population but made up about one-third of those suspended during the 2013–2014 school year.

Discrepancies like these might be termed the "discipline gap"—something distinct from, but analogous to, the achievement gap. They have produced the same sort of controversy as the achievement gap.

The above-cited HHS figures for the school year 1972-73 led the NAACP, the ACLU and many black parents to claim discrimination. They claimed schools were punishing blacks more harshly than whites for the same offenses, and demanded that discipline rates for blacks be cut to match that for whites and Asians. School discipline became a civil rights issue. These critics did not provide evidence that blacks and whites were misbehaving with similar frequency or at similar levels of seriousness. They didn't have to; by the 1970s it had become unchallenged public dogma in the United States that differences between the races were not natural or normal, and could only be caused by differences in treatment, i.e., by discrimination. Where common sense would see evidence of bad behavior on the part of blacks, they saw only mistreatment of blacks.

The same reasoning might lead us to ask whether boys are being specially discriminated against, since they are punished for misbehavior at more than three times the rate for girls. But the denial of sex differences has never gone as unchallenged as the denial of racial differences. Teachers see racial differences in behavior every day, and know just how pervasive and persistent they are. But for many years now, most have feared to discuss the subject openly. One exception is Scott Phelps, a white teacher at John Muir High School in Pasadena, California. In a letter to colleagues that got quoted in the *LA Times* (December 1, 2002), Phelps wrote that unruly black students are responsible for his school's failure to make the grade:

> It has nothing to do with teachers or curriculum.... Overwhelmingly, the students

> whose behavior makes the hallways deafening, who yell out for the teacher and demand immediate attention in class, who cannot seem to stop chatting and are fascinated by each other but not with academics, in short, whose behavior saps the strength and energy of us on the front lines, are African American.

Phelps went on to list white, Hispanic, and Asian teachers who quit because they were intimidated by aggressive black students. Controversy erupted around Mr. Phelps's remarks when they appeared in the *LA Times*, but he kept his job. Today he is president of the Pasadena Unified School District Board of Trustees—proving it is possible to speak honestly about race and survive professionally.

Kitty McKnight is a black graduate of John Muir High School. She sent her two sons there and taught there herself for 40 years. While she acknowledges initial feelings of anger at Phelps' letter, she admits the truth of his observations. When a district official suggested at a public meeting that the solution to Muir's discipline problems was more tolerance and commitment from the teachers, she exploded:

> I cannot sit and listen to this. Our boys are out of control. Having been a teacher all these years, I

> never made it a point. But it's true. You talk about the behavior of black students to another black teacher, and they know exactly what you mean. I feel like I am at fault for not addressing it sooner.

Mrs. McKnight also blamed some of the parents who offer excuses for their kid's bad behavior and have even accused her of being prejudiced against her own race. (Los Angeles *Times,* December 1, 2002)

Pasadena's John Muir is, of course, only one high school. What do the figures look like nationwide?

In South Philadelphia High School, black students have harassed, assaulted and tormented Asian students for years. The black principal explains that they did not alert police because they didn't want to "criminalize" the students.

In Philadelphia as a whole, 409 student assaults on teachers were reported between September 2005 and January 2006. By the 2010-2011 school year, the number had risen to 690 teachers assaulted. The Philadelphia Federation of Teachers, which represents the district's 10,000 teachers, reports that a growing number of its members don't feel safe in their classrooms.

There is reason to fear the official numbers are understated. In 2011, Michael Lodise, president of the school police union, said: "My officers are very frustrated out there because they are being told not to report things and that everything must go through the principal. If he doesn't want to report it, it doesn't get reported." Almost simultaneously, School Superintendent Arlene Ackerman was bragging to the media that violence in the schools had been on the decrease. (*Philadelphia Inquirer*, 28 March 2011)

In Baltimore, 80% of teachers surveyed had been victimized in the workplace according to a survey conducted by the school district in 2011. Over 300 Baltimore teachers filed injury claims from student assaults in 2013.

An article in the American Psychological Association Journal in 2014 stated: "Violence directed against teachers is a national crisis with far-reaching implications and deserves included in the school violence equation" (Dorothy Espelage, PhD, University of Illinois, lead author).

Of the approximately 9,000 arrests and tickets issued to students in Los Angeles during the 2011–2012 school-year, 93 percent involved black and Hispanic students.

Nationwide, black students in 2012 were 15 percent of the student population but they made up more than a third of students suspended once, 44 percent of those suspended more than once, and more than a third of students expelled. Even in preschool, blacks are suspended at two and a half times the average rate. Blacks account for half of students suspended before age 6. (Los Angeles *Times*, 24 March 2014).

The claim that black pupils are unfairly singled out for disciplinary action is alive and well in 21st Century America. In March, 2012 Secretary of Education Arne Duncan called the discrepancy in discipline rates "alarming." "The sad fact," he observed, "is that minority students across America face much harsher discipline than non-minorities even within the same school." In accordance with such thinking, President Obama signed an executive order called the "African American Education Initiative" (26 July 2012). It calls on schools to reduce the number of disciplinary actions against black students. The Civil Rights office has launched investigations in 2012 into several states from North Carolina to Massachusetts on whether discriminatory suspension policies are violating the civil rights of black students.

According to the latest report from the US Department of Education Office of Civil Rights (June 2014), the number of suspensions has dropped across all ethnic groups, with the largest decline being for blacks and Hispanics. Overall suspensions have dropped by 14 percent in the years 2011 to 2014.

Los Angeles Unified Schools brag they have lowered the suspension and expulsion rate. Here is the series of events: In 2011, even before the President's executive order of 2012, the district was found to be in violation of Obama's program according to a Justice Department memo issued in 2010. This prompted Superintendent Deasey to quickly advance a program to reduce discipline actions on all levels and to soften enforcement of rules on non-white student behavior; discipline was said to be "inequitable and disproportionate." In 2012, the district started diverting truant students to counseling at off-site resource centers rather than issue truancy tickets. In 2013, it became the first district in the country to ban suspensions for defiant behavior of students, no matter how bad.

In 2014 the district went even further by eliminating suspension or referral to police for possession of alcohol or less than one gram of marijuana, vandalizing school property or fighting. Sending students to court and putting them on probation has been eliminated for virtually all offenses except carrying guns on campus. No special action is taken against repeat offenders. A school board member who supports the new program indicated on a radio interview (19 August 2014), that no suspensions mean higher attendance, and this will bring more money into the district since the state pays the districts based on attendance. She also said the change will "look good" when the public reviews "social progress" in the schools.

According to LAUSD data for 2013-2014, black students accounted for about 11 percent of the student body but made up about one-third of those suspended even after the initial softening of the enforcement rules.

Los Angeles reduced its rate of suspensions by more than 53 percent by school year 2013-14, but reported crimes and violence in the schools have not decreased. The state government is now pushing directives to reduce the number of suspensions in all districts or force them to explain why this is not possible.

Softening Discipline:

	California		LAUSD	
	Expulsions	**Suspensions**	**Expulsions**	**Suspensions**
2011-12	9553	366,629	152	18,888
2012-13	8226	329,370	128	11,898
2013-14	6611	279,383	145	8864
		Two-Year Decline		
	30.8%	23.8%	4.6%	53.1%

Teachers have complained that the school districts have done too little to help them cope with the resulting discipline problems, which has resulted in classroom disruption at a level not seen before.

The advocacy group Fix School Discipline claims the drop in suspensions and expulsions has lead to higher graduation rates, but produces no evidence of this. Indeed, LAUSD records issued in 2015 said the dropout rate was 17.2% in 2011 and a barely lower 17.0% in 2013. Graduation rate for students in class of 2014 was 70.4%, slightly up from 68.1% the previous year. It is difficult to see these trends as dramatic improvements. Indeed, a UCLA study (11 November 2014) showed that the number of instructional days lost to teacher absences, lockdowns and counseling sessions for disruptive students reached 22.3 in high-poverty areas—the highest figure ever for a school year!

Suspension certainly has its disadvantages as a form of discipline; it involves removing pupils from classes and thus works against a school's fundamental purpose of educating them. But what are the alternatives? In previous years (and even today in many Southern and Midwestern states) paddling of disruptive students was a normal practice. In most of the nation, this is no longer permitted, and suspension was introduced as a substitute.

One new alternative to suspension involves mediation sessions where everyone involved in an incident (teacher, counselor, pupil, and others) gather and talk out the situation for 45 minutes to an hour. While this has reduced suspensions, it may come at the expense of other students who miss the attention of their teachers during such sessions.

Some allege that suspensions mean less education, and that this leads to prison time for many of the offenders later in life. They point out that 82% of those in prison are school drop-outs. In effect, these critics blame school discipline for causing later incarceration.

It seems more likely that tendencies to bad behavior are the cause of both school suspensions during youth, and crime in adulthood. Such tendencies can become visible even before children reach school age. One 16-year study done on 255 men at the federal mental institution in Washington, DC, showed that criminal tendencies show up in kids as young as three. Crime is not caused by discipline or anything else in the environment; it is due to the inability of young men to control anger and emotions. Failure to hold them accountable only encourages their worst tendencies, to the detriment of their peers who want to learn. If current thinking persists, the "discipline gap" is only likely to grow.

FIGURE 4A Anti-social scores of 12-year-olds, by family income quartile

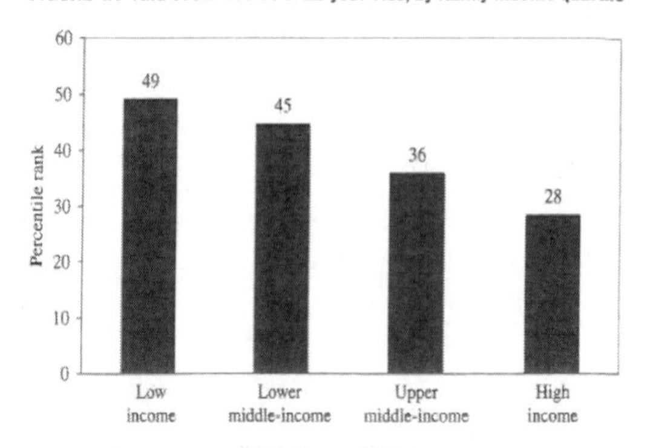

Source: Carneiro and Heckman (2002); Masterov (2004).

FIGURE 4B Anti-social scores of 12-year-olds, by race

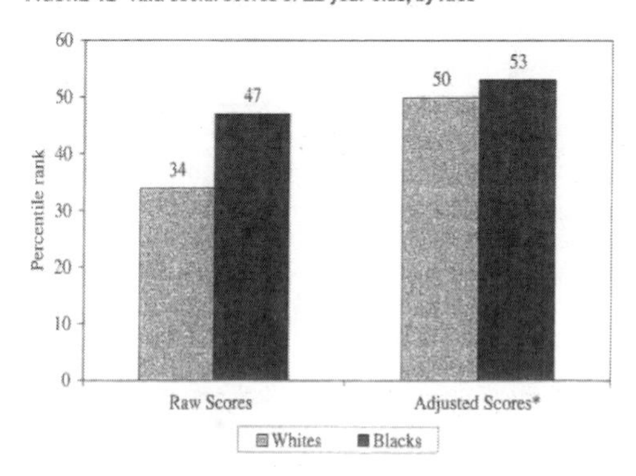

* Anti-social scores of black and white 12-year-olds whose family income, family structure, and mother's education are similar.

Source: Carneiro and Heckman (2002); Masterov (2004).

FIGURE 4C Anti-social scores, by race, from 4 years old to 12 years old*

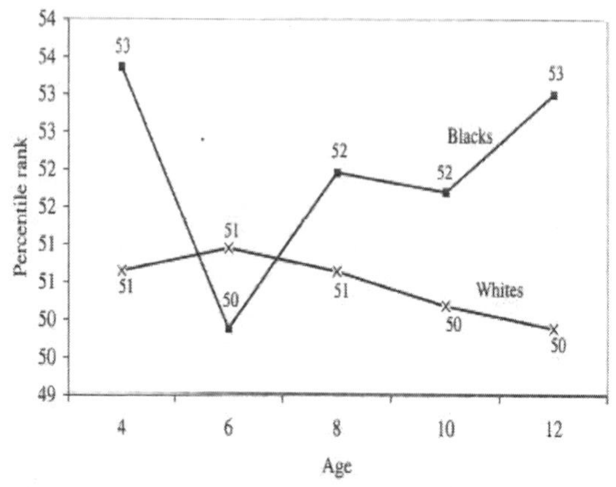

* Anti-social scores of black and white children, at ages 4, 6, 8, 10, and 12, whose family income, family structure, and mother's education are similar.

Source: Carneiro and Heckman (2002), Mastcrov (2004).

FIGURE 4D Anti-social scores, by family income quartile, from 4 years old to 12 years old*

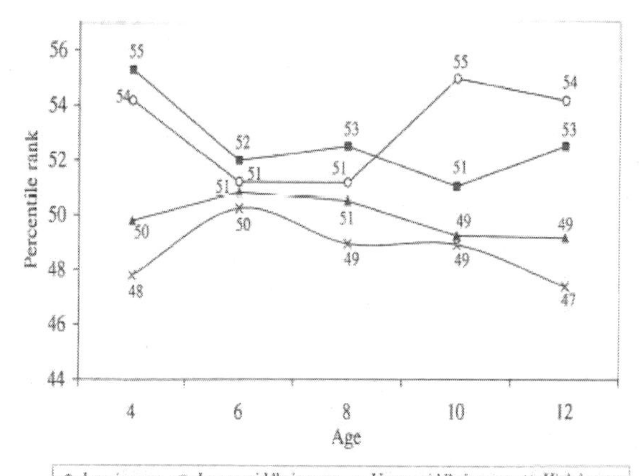

* Anti-social scores of black and white children, at ages 4, 6, 8, 10, and 12, whose family income, family structure, and mother's education are similar.

Source: Carneiro and Heckman (2002), Masterov (2004).

xiv

GENETICS: THE ELEPHANT IN THE ROOM

Despite the billions spent by government and philanthropy in the past fifty years for preschools, better classroom environments and general socioeconomic uplift, there has been no change in average academic achievement by race in the United States.

The race gap in America is comparable to that of other countries as well. In South Africa, e.g., 96 percent of white students pass their high school exit exams. The passing rate for blacks was 42 percent. In Soweto, the nation's largest black community, it was ten percent. (Los Angeles *Times* story April 21, 1990)

Reality has been defined as that which continues to exist when you stop believing in it. Several decades ago, Americans officially ceased considering racial differences natural or normal. In our Tried But Failed chapter, we listed forty proposed alternative explanations for observed differences in the average academic achievement of the races in America, with corresponding reform proposals intended to make such differences go away. None has proven successful.

It is time to reconsider a tacit assumption behind all such efforts: viz., that without some form of unfairness or discrimination, all races would, on average, succeed in school to the same extent. No one has ever demonstrated why this should be the case. As economist Walter Williams puts it:

> There is no evidence from anywhere on earth or any time in human history which demonstrates that but for discrimination there would be proportional representation and absence of gross statistical disparities by race, sex, nationality or any other human characteristic. (Diversity, Ignorance and Stupidity, 2012)

The world is filled with differences not attributable to discrimination: diseases specific to certain groups (e.g., Tay-Sachs to Askenazi Jews, Sickle Cell to blacks), the overwhelmingly white population of Maine, wealthy people attending more opera or going to more art galleries than poor people, etc. These disparities do not prove discrimination or imply any injustice that would require remedial action.

To take an example from professional sports: it is no more scandalous that few blacks become professional hockey players or NASCAR drivers than that blacks dominate the NBA. Such differences are quite normal. In part they may be due to free choices people make, e.g., young blacks taking more interest in basketball than hockey, and sometimes they reflect natural differences, as when blacks dominate international sprinting competitions because of their higher proportion of fast-twitch muscle tissue.

Blacks even excel whites in certain mental abilities. They outperform whites at the same IQ level in rote learning tasks, and develop motor skills earlier. However, they have less tissue in the pre-frontal cortex, which translates into poorer abstract reasoning and lower IQ. This is not a recent discovery; experts have known it for many decades. (*Scientific Study* by Helmuth Nyberg, 2009). It remains undiscussed partly out of fear and partly because many who know the truth think that suppressing information about racial differences will somehow make racial problems disappear or protect the self-esteem of blacks.

The ultimate cause of natural differences in living organisms is found in DNA, the genetic code of life. Science has increasingly found that genes have a huge impact on what humans (like other animals) are and can become. Other factors play a role: it is important to get proper nutrition, especially in the early years and in the mother's womb, and brain injuries or drug use may obviously limit one's ability to learn and achieve. Our genes, however, appear largely to determine the maximum we can achieve when all other circumstances are favorable; poor nutrition, injuries and drug abuse all lower our potential, but virtually nothing has been found to raise our potential as determined by our genes.

Several lines of argument agree in supporting the genetic hypothesis. Perhaps the most striking evidence comes from twin studies. Identical twins share the same genome; in other words, *all* their genes are identical. Occasionally, such twins get separated at birth and are raised in very different environments. Researchers study such twin pairs to determine the degree to which intelligence is determined by genes. More than two hundred such pairs of twins have been studied since the 1930s. The best and most extensive such studies were carried out by Thomas Bouchard and his colleagues at the University of Minnesota, beginning in 1979. Bouchard's team found that intelligence is 83 percent heritable. They also determined that "relevant environmental influences are unique to the individual rather than operating as family effects arising from shared or common family influences such as parental styles or upbringing, discipline, role models, encouragement, and the like." (Richard Lynn, *The Science of Human Diversity* (Lanham: UPA, 2011) 297-306)

Another way of investigating the relative influence of genetics and environment is by looking at transracial adoptions. The most important such study was carried out by Bouchard's University of Minnesota colleagues Sandra Scarr and Richard A. Weinberg beginning in the 1970s; it is known as the Minnesota Transracial Adoption Study.

In the United States, most transracial adoptions involve black or mixed-race children adopted by white couples. In the Minnesota study, the adoptive parents were mostly college graduates employed in managerial and professional occupations. All adoptees were given IQ tests and scholastic tests at ages seven and seventeen. At age seven, the adopted children showed IQs several points higher than the average for blacks raised in a black family. This would suggest their environment had a significant impact on them. At age 17, however, the black group did not score significantly higher than blacks raised in a black family—i.e., about sixteen points below the white average. The children from a white mother and black father tested in the mid-range of eight points below the average white student on a national basis. The study concluded that the effects of a favorable environment fade with time, and that adult intelligence depends mostly on genes. (General Cognitive Ability-g factor article in Assessment,

Encyclopedia Psychological Assessment, a Sage Publication 2000).

These results have been confirmed by similar studies carried out in Sweden. The Swedish Adoption/Twin Study of Aging provided corroborative data for high heritability. Studied were 45 pairs of identical twins reared apart, 67 pairs of identical twins raised together, 100 pairs of fraternal twins reared apart, and 89 pairs of fraternal twins reared together, all with an average age of 65. The heritability of general intelligence was found to be about 80%, somewhat lower for specific abilities. Thus, average heritabilities for verbal, spatial and memory tests were repectively 58%, 46% and 38% (Pedersen, Plomin, Nesselroade, and Mc Learn, *Intelligence*, 6 July 1992).

A more recent study investigated American armed forces veterans in their late 30s; the men were fairly representative of the black and white male population. The results indicated that when black and whites are matched on g scores "there is no evidence of discrimination unfavorable to blacks for job status at any level of g. Nor are blacks with the same g scores as whites disadvantaged in income when they are above the median level of g in the total the total sample. In fact, on both variables - job status and income - whites turned out to be relatively more disadvantaged group when the level of g is taken into account." (Helmuth Nyborg and Arthur Jensen, "Occupation and Income Related to Psychometric g," *Intelligence*, 20 October 1999).

These examples could be multiplied. A host of distinguished scientists, including Arthur Jensen, William Shockley, J. Philippe Rushton, Richard Lynn, Hans Eysenck, Philip Vernon, Sandra Scarr, and many others, have tried to tell us the scientific facts about genetic differences. All were brilliant, and held appointments at prestigious universities. Many have been shouted down while attempting to address university audiences, or have been subjected to libelous personal attacks from professional "anti-racists." The weight of their research and studies has simply been ignored by the media and America's political leadership. There is probably no other area in which expert opinion and popular understanding are farther apart. As far back as 1984, scholars Mark Snyderman and Stanley Rothman surveyed more than 600 experts in the field of psychological measurement. Responses were anonymous. Most believed that IQ tests measured the ability to solve problems and to reason abstractly, and that heredity accounted for much of the variation between racial groups. Yet the impression given in the popular press was that intelligence could not be defined, that IQ tests do not measure anything that is relevant to life performance and that aptitude tests are outmoded and useless—all in direct contradiction to the results of their survey. They published their findings in 1988 as *The IQ Controversy*. Not much seems to have changed since then. Herrnstein and Murray's 1994 book *The Bell Curve* received considerable publicity when it was published, and was read by many people, but the evidence they presented was prevented from having any influence on public policy. It is doubtful such a work could even be published today.

Some would have us believe that IQ and achievement tests are culturally biased. There is an organization called FairTest which campaigns against standardized testing for this reason. They like to bring up a SAT question which required knowledge of the term "regatta," but are not as quick to mention that this item has not appeared since 1973. Test designers today are keenly aware of the issue of cultural bias and put a great deal of effort into minimizing its effects. Most IQ tests today are non-verbal for this very reason. The current leader in the field of IQ testing is Raven's Progressive Matrices, which require no reading at all. An example is given in the illustration below:

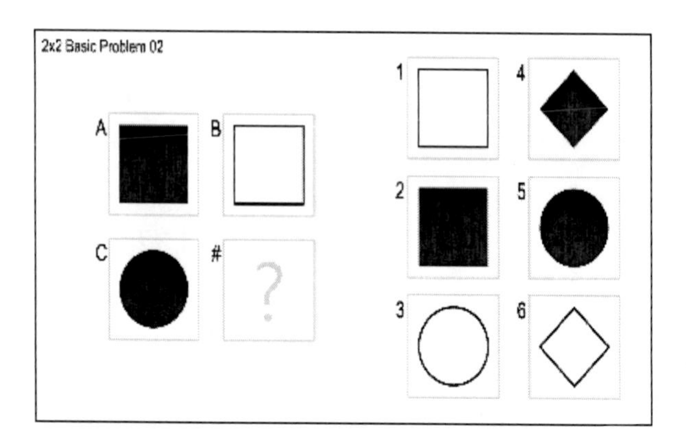

A typical problem from a modern IQ test: find the shape on the right that best fits in the empty space on the left.

Of course in a sense, all tests "discriminate"—that is their purpose. An IQ test, e.g., is meant to discriminate between different levels of intelligence; a third grade math test is meant to identify those who have learned the material from those who have not. Such tests are not intended to discriminate against races *as such*, but if there are differences between the average ability of the races, good tests will reveal them.

We might also point out that liberal egalitarian policy-makers are happy to appeal to IQ testing when it suits them. For example:

1. IQ tests determine who can get into the military; no one under 80 IQ is allowed to join per a Congressional rule.
2. The Supreme Court has mandated that anyone with an IQ less than 70 cannot be executed, no matter the crime.
3. Admission to special education is set by IQ level as directed by the various States.

Of course, some egalitarians would have all such tests banned. A federal judge has forbidden IQ testing of blacks in the state of California since 1979. In 2003, the NAACP filed a federal complaint against Florida's Education Department in an effort to prevent the use of statewide assessment tests until the achievement gap between minority students and white students is eliminated.

The Academic Performance Index (API) exam, which is the national norm in testing and one used for progress analysis, allows minorities to meet only 80 percent of the targets set for everyone else. Call it "institutional racism," said Jim Lanich, President of California Business for Education Excellence. (*Mountain News*, 20 April 2006)

A "resource guide" published by the US Department of Education's Office of Civil Rights in 1999 states that "any use of any education test (such as the SAT or ACT) which has a significant disparate impact on members of any particular race, national origin, or sex is discriminatory" and should be viewed as invalid unless the school using the test can prove otherwise. By this standard, no test is valid. (John Leo, *US News*, 31 May 1999)

But would subjective standards bring fairness to admissions or evaluations?

The study of group differences is not designed to harm persons of any particular race. Such study is more likely to make it possible to adapt our educational approach to different racial groups and different levels of ability.

Where did these differences come from? Why aren't all races of mankind equally endowed? The explanation accepted by most scientists is based upon the different conditions that prevail in different regions of the world. Our species originated in tropical Africa, where there are no winters and food is plentiful at all times of the year. From there, man spread out across the continents of Asia and Europe. The colder climates he encountered meant that food was no longer equally available at all times of the year; man was forced to plan ahead in order to survive the winter. Those who were not intelligent or future-oriented enough to do so were not able to pass their genes on to posterity. So the average intelligence of men in Asia and Europe gradually rose, while in Africa itself, it tended to remain the same.

Some may object that I lay unnecessary stress on racial differences, whereas the important point is to treat each child as an individual. I can only respond that I am hardly the first person to suggest racial comparisons; such comparisons are an obsession of liberal egalitarians, be they politicians, journalists, or education leaders. They are the ones who constantly talk about the "gap" between the races and the supposed need to close it. And yet as I have tried to point out in this work, nothing has worked to do this. Nothing in 50 years! I am happy to see each child assessed individually—I only ask that differences in group averages be recognized as natural and normal.

Here are some ways in which American education might be improved through the recognition of natural differences:

1. End racial preferences. They are unfair to whites and Asians, and they deprive their black and Hispanic "beneficiaries" of incentive to achieve. They produce underqualified professionals who shortchange or harm those who employ their services, and they reinforce the very "stereotypes" of

low black performance they are intended to combat. At first introduced in a rather shamefaced way as a temporary remedy that would be abolished when no longer needed, they have perpetuated themselves by their very failure, and are a powerful cause of resentment among both "beneficiaries" and victims.

2. End the culture of victimhood so widespread among blacks in this country. Blacks from Africa and the Caribbean do much better in their studies here than native blacks, possibly because they have been less influenced by the victim mentality common in America. Yes, black Americans have had more than their share of trouble in the past, but they are in no way helped by being encouraged to blame their problems on others in the present.

3. Bring back ability grouping. As far as practicable, teach according to each student's ability regardless of race. Encourage blacks to become the best *black* people they can be, rather than remaining preoccupied with inappropriate and invidious comparisons with whites.

4. Some of the money currently being spent on vain efforts to raise the achievement levels of the most poorly performing students should be redirected toward helping the gifted and talented. This group is

the most overlooked today, although it includes most of those who will be responsible for future progress and leadership. In the past, the most naturally gifted received *most* help for just this reason.

5. Stop forcing all students to take college prep courses. Not everyone is suited to college. It makes no sense to ruin a good plumber for the sake of creating a bad lawyer. Low academic achievers must be guided into trades or other blue collar (skilled or semi-skilled) jobs where they can succeed, rather than being forced into college prep where they are bound to fail. Classes in subjects like woodworking, auto repair, metal crafts, etc., should be restored to their rightful place in the high school curriculum. Thousands of young people who might succeed in such trades are presently being made to feel like failures. Either they flunk college prep and drop out of high school, or they barely pass, go to college, and fail there or get bogged down in remedial courses. Up to 45 percent of incoming American freshmen require remedial courses in math, writing, and reading (Walter Williams, *Education Today*, 2014); and 80 percent of college students taking remedial classes in 2008 had a high school Grade Point Average of 3.0 or better (*Washington Times*, November 2011). Students often end up with crippling amounts of debt and no job. (Total debt for

college loans is fast approaching one trillion dollars, with seven million ex-students in default.) According to a recent study by Wells Fargo in 2014, one-third of Millennials (18 to 34 years old) say they would have been better off working than attending college.

The current system is highly lucrative for the education establishment, but how does it help young people contribute to society or get the most out of life?

6. End uncontrolled immigration from countries with low average intelligence levels (IQ) such as Mexico (average IQ: 87). Young people from such countries add to the already large number of low-achieving students with which our schools are dealing so ineffectually. We have over 18 million illegal immigrants in this country (a conservative estimate), aside from an even larger number of legal immigrants; most haven't finished high school, and many can't read English. So what are we doing to ourselves? Where will they all fit in the future job market in the U.S.? Are we not really just building a permanent underclass by all these actions and failures?

Statistical projections based on current immigration patterns indicate that the US Population in 2050 will consist of 13% blacks, 29% Hispanics, 47% whites and 9% Asians. According to scholar Byron Roth, population projections and IQ estimates for these various groups suggest that the overall IQ of the US population will fall from about 98 today to about 95 by mid-century. The effects will be greatest among the most intelligent. If we set the IQ necessary for receiving college instruction at 110—a generous estimate—then the percentage of qualifying young people in the US will fall from 21% today to 16% in 2050—a decline of 24% at a time when advanced training is becoming increasingly important. More demanding jobs such as doctors, research scientists, etc. require a minimum IQ of 120. This group will decline from 7.1% to 4.8%—a huge drop.

For comparative purposes, consider that an increasingly aggressive and self-confident China will in 2050 have some 160 million people out of 1.2 billion with an IQ over 120, while the U.S. will have only 20 million out of 320 million people—a ratio of eight to one. (Roth, *The Perils of Diversity*, 470-473) How will America keep its level of prosperity and strength given these trends?

We must heed the warning of Dr. Arthur Jensen on the importance of general intelligence (g) in a complex, industrialized, information-intensive society:

> It would be difficult to see how a society with only 1% of its population above IQ 120 could maintain a complex, technologically advanced system. Those with higher intelligence should be encouraged to have more children when in fact they now have less. Immigration by those with low skills or intelligence should be replaced by those whose skills are needed in science, computer and engineering fields. (*Giftedness and Genius: Crucial Differences*)

7. Enforce discipline fairly but effectively. Students cannot learn in a hostile or violent environment in the schools. Students differ in their need for discipline just as they do in achievement, so racial quotas for suspensions or other punishments are not appropriate.

8. Stop shielding incompetent teachers with tenure.

9. Allow parents to choose their children's schools. Freedom of choice in education, with variety and competition among methods of schools, is more likely to result in successful programs than a centrally dominated system.

10. End Federal mandating of educational programs for neighborhood schools.

Why do so many Americans refuse to recognize natural differences? Because in our culture, the concept of civic equality has been twisted into a denial of natural inequality. Equality is a principle that can be applied within the context of human institutions: equality before the law, one-man-one-vote, etc. As Snyderman and Rothman write in The IQ Controversy:

> The danger inherent in egalitarianism is that a philosophy of human rights may be extrapolated into a theory of human nature. That individuals should be treated equally does not mean that all individuals are equal. Whether as a result of accidents of birth and environment, or through strength of will, people differ in abilities of all sorts.

An educational system that recognizes individual and group differences as normal will be adaptable to the needs of different students, better enabling each of them to fulfill their potential. Educational fairness should not mean the *same* program of instruction for every child, but an equal opportunity to excel in appropriately different programs tailored to individual differences in general ability and specific aptitudes. Life satisfaction is not the product of extensive education and advanced degrees but from doing one's personal best and achieving a place in society—even if, for most of us, it is a modest place.

STAR test results

The proficiency gap between California's white, Latino, and black students has remained almost unchanged even as their test scores have improved.

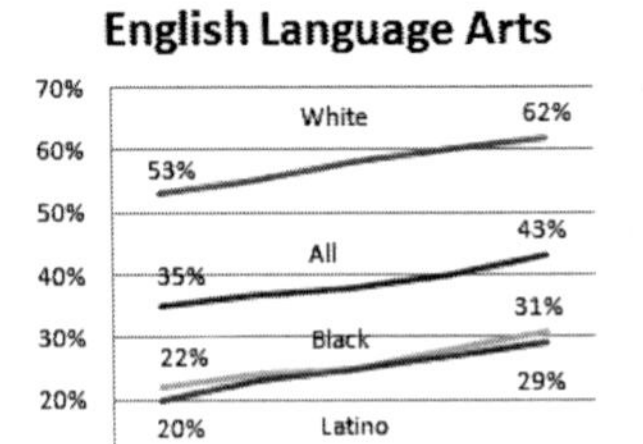

Mathmatics

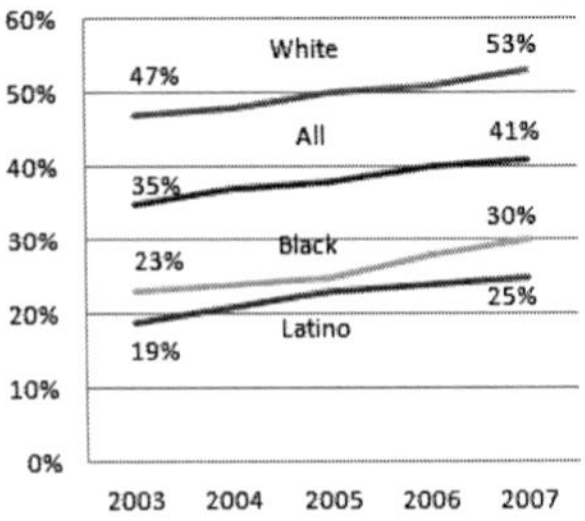

Note: 2007 scores are preliminary
Source: California Department of Education

Index xv

AN APPENDIX – EDUCATION TODAY

APPENDIX 1:

Racial Comparisons

When making racial comparisons in educational achievement and test scores in the United States, it is customary to distinguish four groups: whites, blacks, Hispanics (also known as Latinos) and Asians. These categories were not arrived at in any rational or systematic way. Hispanics are not even a racial category at all, but include persons of any race who trace their ancestry back to a Spanish speaking country. In large parts of the US, the great majority of "Hispanics" are Mexican mestizos, a mixture of American Indian and European. But in New York City, most "Hispanics" are Puerto Rican, while in South Florida, many are Cuban. Obviously, comparisons between such different groups are of limited value.

High Asian achievement and test scores are mainly due to persons of Chinese, Japanese and Korean ancestry. But the term "Asian" also includes Pacific Islanders, who now number 1.2 million in the United States and have not done well in school. Only 18 percent have a bachelor's degree, similar to the figures for Hispanics and blacks. The Hmong and Khmer communities from South East Asia also tend to lower achievement scores for "Asians," as do, to a lesser extent, Vietnamese Americans.

Even "white" is a problematic category. As defined by the US Census bureau, "white" people include Arabs, Iranians and persons from the Indian subcontinent. Representatives of these groups have protested their inclusion in the "white" category, but so far the law has not been changed. If the "white" category were restricted to persons of European origin, average "white" academic achievement and test scores would rise somewhat, thus widening the achievement gap.

All these classifications are a matter of political convenience, having nothing to do with physical anthropology or social reality.

High School GPA (Males): Disaggregation for Asian Groups

Race/Ethnicity	June 2000	June 2001	June 2002
Cambodian	1.67	1.79	1.80
Chinese	3.52	3.90	3.82
Hmong	1.80	2.15	2.00
Japanese	3.70	3.95	3.75
Korean	3.31	3.50	3.73
Lao	1.9	2.00	2.50
Vietnamese	3.40	3.60	3.83
All Asian Males	**2.76**	**2.98**	**3.06**

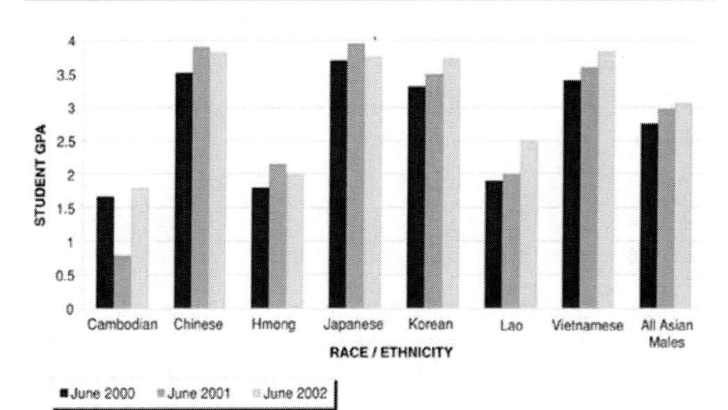

NOTE: Sample data based on 4.0 scale.

Index xvi

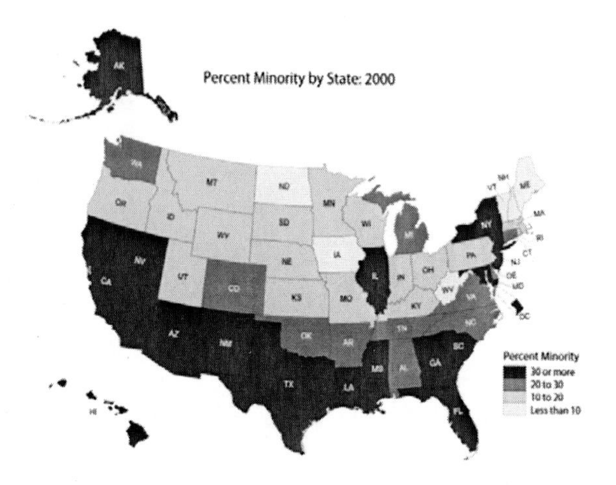

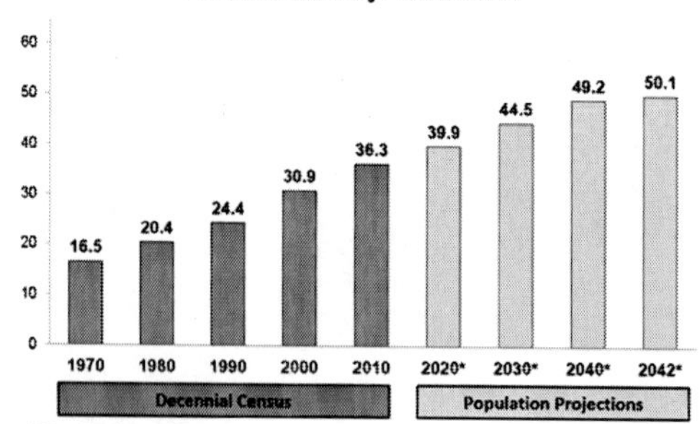

*Projected population as of July 1.
Note: "Minority" refers to people who reported their ethnicity and race as something other than non-Hispanic White alone in the decennial census.

Source: U.S. Census Bureau, decennial census of population, 1970 (5-percent sample), 1980 to 2010, 2008 Population Projections, 2020-2042.

Index xvii

APPENDIX 2:
Special Education Cost and Reality

America's special education system today is a far cry from what Congress envisioned when it passed the path-breaking IDEA(Individual with Disabilities Act) legislation in 1975. Disabled children, the law's sponsors vowed, would be guaranteed a "free appropriate public education". They envisioned such children being taught alongside of students in the general population with special aids and support as needed. Washington promised the states that it would reimburse them 40% of the cost incurred to education handicapped children. In reality this was never more than 7% and such a shortfall has left many states bitter about the mandated program. Then in 1993, the US Supreme Court ordered a South Carolina district to reimburse the family of a learning disabled child for tuition paid to send the youngster to a private school because the family felt the public school was not providing the level of education mandated. About one in four special education students drop out of school and those who graduate remain unemployed an average of 3-5 years. And nearly one third- primarily those with emotional disabilities-are arrested at least once after leaving high school.

The costs in some cases are staggering. In California, a school system had to pay $188,000 to send an emotionally disturbed student to a Texas psychiatric institution for 14 months. A Georgia school system paid $42,000 toward the cost of sending a mentally retarded student to Japan for "special education." In some cases the outside referrals are needed where a school district can't provide what the law requires, but many times the parents put the child in a private school and then sue the district to cover the costs. They usually win since it has been shown that achievement scores do rise when private, expensive education is obtained by the parents where the child then received individualized attention that these schools can provide. (US News and World Report, December 13, 1993)

APPENDIX 3:
Reading Gap Widens in Past Ten Years

In nearly every state, the reading gap between lower and higher income students increased. In 12 states and the District of Columbia, the gap widened by more than 30% with the largest increases in DC, Hawaii and Tennessee. Disparities are also apparent among the five largest racial groups. According to the 2013 study published by the Annie Casey Foundation, a very liberal organization, 83% of black students, 81% of Latinos, 78% of American Indian, 55% of white students and 49% of Asian students are not proficient in the reading skills.

They refer to data from the US Department of Education, National Center for Educational Statistics, National Assessment of Educational Progress (NAEP), 2013 Reading Assessment.

By 2020, the United States is expected to face a shortage of 1.5 million workers with college degrees and a surplus of 6 million unemployed people without a high school diploma.

In an article in the Los Angeles *Times*, July 18, 2015, Howard Blum stated that No Child Left Behind had an ambitious goal to reform America's schools in 16 years; "Every student, everywhere, would be academically successful by 2014. This hasn't happened and the vast majority of schools that receive federal aid are now labeled as failures under the law."

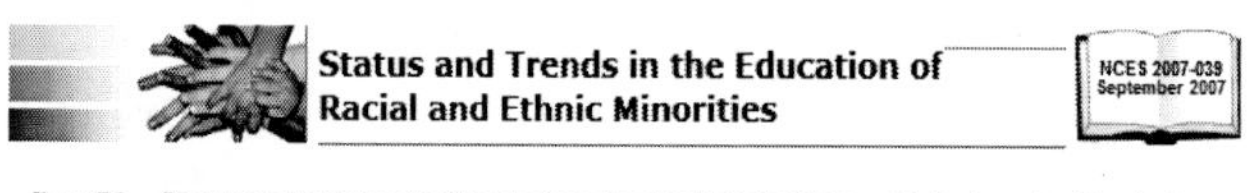

Figure 7.3. Percentage distribution of public school enrollment in the United States and in five largest public school districts, by race/ethnicity: 2004

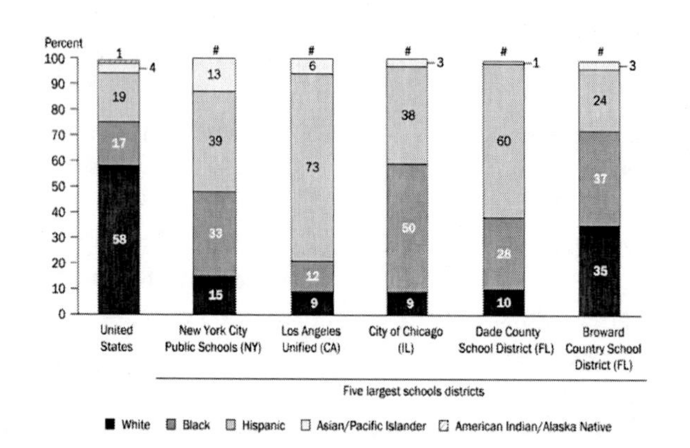

Rounds to zero.

NOTE: Broward County School District was the sixth largest school district in 2004, but is included here because the fifth largest school district, Clark County, did not report race/ethnicity data in 2004. Race categories exclude persons of Hispanic origin. Detail may not sum to totals because of rounding.

SOURCE: U.S. Department of Education, National Center for Education Statistics, The NCES Common Core of Data (CCD), "Public Elementary/Secondary School Universe Survey," 2004–05.

Index xviii

APPENDIX 4:
Athletics and Academics

The University of Maryland is the only American university that links athletic coaches' compensation to the academic performance of student athletes. In January 2015, University of California trustees debated the introduction of a similar policy. However, Board of Regents member Eddie Island argued that UC "should not impose a cultural arrogance by setting grade and class standards too high for athletes. We ought not to put harmful stumbling blocks in the way of young people's dreams of pro careers," he said. The University delayed a decision. Tying coach salaries to the academic achievement of their athletes (that can run as much as $3.5 million per year) might drive away top dollar coaches and require that their team members actually learn something tangible in college. Thus the fear at the UC Regents meeting was that rigorous academic requirements might force students to take the least demanding classes or leave UC for a college without such rules. (Larry Gordon, *LA Times*, 16 January 2015).

Here is another good example of the impact of special consideration for winning ball teams in this country. Notre Dame dismissed four football starters for academic fraud in August 2014; no further details were given. All were allowed to eventually return. The same was true when the quarterback who was suspended in 2013 for cheating on tests was allowed to return to the team. This as Notre Dame tried to hold onto its number 17 position in the coaches' poll.

The University of North Carolina has admitted its academic-fraud-for-athletes scandal was worse than the public had been told. It is now known that over the past 18 years, some 3,100 students took "paper classes" with no faculty oversight and no actual class attendance. Black Studies had hosted *all* the fake classes. Black athletes were promised that their work on the sports teams would lead to *real* education. (*Bloomberg Businessweek,* 22 October 2014)

APPENDIX 5:
Cheating to Raise Test Scores

There have been many school districts and unique classes that have shown spectacular improvement in the past few years. This is far in excess of what one might expect and way above the norm. So these were used by liberals to verify that special teaching, special classes, special love can work wonders. And while some success stories do exist they are usually with surrounding circumstances that distort the generalizations being made (such as most of the parents were college grads, all had to enroll in special magnet schools and commit to total involvement, etc).

Sadly many of these 'success' stores are clouded with cheating by teachers and administrators on a rather massive scale in some areas. Here are some examples:

1. Mrs. MiSawna Moore, principal in a school in Charleston, South Carolina was given awards and lauded for the tremendous improvements she brought to her school in a black neighborhood. She is now under investigation for criminal fraud, and when tested this year, only 44% of her students could meet the state standard, vs. 84.6 the previous year. Most of the

tests had erasures on them and this led to the investigation.

2. Pennsylvania's top prosecutor has charged a principal and four teachers with helping students cheat on their exams.

3. In Las Vegas, an investigation was started after a dramatic increase in test scores in 2011-12 in Kelly Elementary School. The principal and three others were fired when a large number of errors on the answer sheet had been obviously changed.

4. Twenty Seven schools in California lost their test rankings this past year including five in Los Angeles city due to the discovery of widespread cheating on tests used to gauge student performance and achievement. Schools are in Compton, Pasadena, Burbank, Lancaster and Torrance. Teachers would in some cases call the students to their desks to review the answers and give them the corrected ones. One math teacher put the questions and answers on the black board.

5. Carpenter Charter School near Studio City, Los Angeles has long been considered a top

performer. Last year they averaged 941 on the Academic Performance index which is based on standardized tests and easily passed the state's target of 800. It was found that over 120 addresses of students attending could not be verified and it was determined that they had imported kids from surrounding areas so that the scores could be boosted.

6. In 2011 the State of California threw out the test scores of a top-performing Los Angeles school and of the highest scoring campus in the Green Dot charter school program after it was found out that several teachers had aided the students to cheat on their tests.

7. According to a report in 2011, in the Atlanta school system, 182 educators have admitted cheating with misconduct documented at 44 of 100 schools. They then agreed to pay back $363,000 in federal money won by teachers and administrators for the great job they had been doing. (reported in the LA Times January 16, 2012). Then 35 educators and administrators were indicted for racketeering and corruption. A sad end to a district that was once touted as the model for the nation to follow for urban school districts. This included Beverly Hall, former

schools superintendent who gained national recognition in 2009 for turning the district around. Turned out that she was the ring leader in the deliberate cheating process in the district. She even terminated teachers who reported they had seen cheating in the previous few years (2005 to 2009). She passed away last year before her codefendants were sentenced to prison terms of up to seven years.

8. In Washington DC, several school scores and tests have been held in abeyance after it was learned of widespread cheating by teachers trying to circumvent the tough policies of the new supervisor, Michelle Rhee. In 2010, the testing company suggested an investigation was in order when the erasure rates at 103 of its 168 schools were thought to be excessive. Rhee was reluctant to investigate do fearing it might blemish her merit pay program where principals at eight schools with such high erasures had just been given an annual bonus of up to $10,000 for boosting student test scores by an average of 48 points.

9. Short Avenue Elementary school, Arlington, Texas, which until now had been touted as a success story. They are overwhelmingly Latino

and two-thirds are low income. Last year the school's ranking was 848 before the cheating scandal which basically saw teachers either filling in the right answers or walking around the class pointing out wrong answers during the test.

10. Crescendo, which operates six schools in South LA, recently had its founder, John Allen, fired after the district uncovered widespread test cheating in the mostly black community. Seals were broken on the tests received which allowed the teachers to then train the students on the answers some days before the tests were given.

11. According to a report by US News and World Report, 35% of teachers surveyed in North Carolina in 1990 admitted they were aware of or involved with test tampering. In a national survey of teachers, one in 11 reported pressure from administrators to cheat on the standardized tests.

12. Cherokee Elementary School in Lake Forest, IL was riding high in the late 1980s. Named one of the nation's outstanding elementary schools by the US Department of Education, principal Linda Chase won kudos as a leading principal. Superintendent Allen Klingenberg was honored

as one of the nation's top 100 educators and named Superintendent of the Year. Then the truth came out. Both had urged teachers to doctor their students' scores in order to inflate Cherokee's reputation.

13. Public School 5 on Staten Island, NY had the highest reading scores in the borough for 5 straight years, an accomplishment that earned them lavish praise. Turns out that the school's principal, Murray Brenner, had systematically changed students incorrect answers. The story broke when a mother of a disabled child reported that he had scored 90% on the tests but could barely speak a full sentence.

14. Under a 1989 Oklahoma law, schools are put on probation by the state if their students' average scores on the Iowa Test of Basic Skills rank in the bottom fourth statewide. In 1991, 121 schools worked their way off the state's probation list by raising their scores. Then it was discovered that the tactic used was to have the test be taken only by the brightest in the class. Two or three students in all these schools had been exempted under the state loophole that say special-education children can be excused from the test with parent's permission.

15. A similar incident occurred in Mission Viejo, CA at Oxford Preparatory Academy. They had scored in their first year of operation in 2012 a near perfect score of 993 out of 1000. Parents reported being asked by their teachers to keep their low performing kids home the day of the tests and many did.

16. In 2008, teacher assistant Johanna Munoz helped her Orlando area fourth graders on the state achievement tests. She erased wrong answers and whispered corrections while she was helping non-native English speakers with difficult words. She snapped her fingers in a code students understood they should correct an answer. While the teacher was out of the room, she warned all the kids "don't tell anyone, not even your parents." If they told, she warned, they 'would fail the 4th grade."

17. In an Arizona State University survey published in 2010, more than 50% of teachers admitted to some kind of cheating on Arizona's tests. They included a base of 3000 teachers who defined cheating broadly—from accidentally leaving multiplication tables on the board, to changing answers directly on the tests.

18. In Pontiac MI, a state investigation concluded the executive director of K-12 instruction in the district "assisted students in changing answers" while proctoring tests in 4th grade math and language tests at Crofort Elementary in 2005. In 2003 this school tested 39% proficient, in 2005 it reached 100%. On the English tests, 80% of them had erasures that changed the answers from wrong to right.

19. In 2008 state writing tests at rural Jefferson County Middle School in Florida were summoned to the cafeteria for a surprise practice test. Turns out the questions matched the tests given the next day for real. The discussion on who blew the whistle got heated at times since the principal was black and the superintendent was white. In the latest test given on what is presumed a fair basis, the average rank was a D. The year before the cheating incident their rank was an F. In the year of the cheating the score stood at a B.

20. Harvard reports that 62% of undergraduate students admitted to cheating on either tests or papers, according to Rutgers professor who studies student attitudes (2011)

21. Student photos of many state standardized tests are being posted on social media as cell phones become more prevalent. This has caused a two week delay in the release of scores for nearly 150 schools in California according to an article in the LA Times July 19, 2012. Some of the schools affected are Millikan High in Long Beach, and North Hollywood High. In all, 249 students posted 442 images on social-networking sites. The 147 affected schools are spread across 94 districts.

22. A Westside charter school teacher, in California, has left her job following allegations that she pointed out wrong answers to her 4th grade class students. Ocean Charter enrolls about 420 students and has two locations: Del Rey and Mar Vista.

23. Investigators with the State Department of Education found that Maryland School Assessment scores were compromised at Abbottston Elementary and Ft. Washington Elementary in 2009 and 2010. The disclosure marks the second time in little more than a year that city school officials have had to acknowledge cheating at schools recognized

nationally as models of successful urban education, including one visited by Michelle Obama and another visited by the US Secretary of Education and held up as models for the nation to follow. At one school unfinished test books were completed by the teachers and at the other there was an alarming incidence of erasures.

24. New York City officials invalidated scores on Regents high school math exams and math tests in grades three through eight in Uniondale District. Staffers were found to alter the tests after taken. The next year the school test scores fell dramatically in contrast with most of Long Island.

25. In Texas, the Dallas Morning News claimed there are more than 50,000 cases of cheating on the Texas Assessment of Knowledge and Skills. Nearly a third of the schools in Texas were found to have allowed some form of cheating including students copying each other's tests.

26. The Dayton, OH Daily News asked the state why no notice had been taken of the fact that the City Day Charter School, which ranked last in the state on the 2005 state math test, outranked

> the highest scoring schools in the state in 2006. They found that 44 questions from the exam had been given the students before the tests were given.

And this is only a partial report on the sad state of today's schools and the supposed success of the various programs to close the educational gap and raise student scores.

APPENDIX 6:
Colleges Rethink Placement Tests

Placement tests are designed for applying students to take so that the college knows what remedial classes they should require of that new student. However, some of the educated elite at these colleges are pushing for an elimination of most of these remedial classes since they cost the poor students money, take time to complete and may discourage them to the point of their dropping out. No mention is made of the need for these students who performed poorly in high school to have the necessary skills to even attempt college level work.

Judith Scott-Clayton, author of a recent study on remedial placement by the Community College Research Center at Teachers College, Columbia University, says that placement tests are a poor indicator of how students will perform in college classes and that high school grade point averages can be a better barometer. I found this an odd comment given the rampant grade inflation found in most schools and the that fact that many students can now graduate with a D average.

Connecticut has just passed legislation to replace most remedial education at public colleges with intensive college-readiness programs and supplemental support.

California law requires the use of multiple criteria, such as test scores, study skills, educational background and goals, to determine in which classes to place students in. But the placement test is the primary tool; transcripts and grade point averages are not widely used.

And now Long Beach City College has launched a program called, Promise Pathways, which could provide a model for the entire system of 112 community colleges in the state of California. They will use high school grades in English and math classes along with transcripts to determine the appropriate college classes which students must take in their first semester. It is assumed to cut by a third the number of students having to take remedial classes. This is not totally clear. This is expected to "especially benefit black and Latino students, who are disproportionately assigned to remedial classes," said Long Beach City College President Eloy Oakley.

Students in the program will also have to enroll in a college success course to help them with time management, note-taking, and other study skills.

"If students can start at a higher level, their chances of success are going to be far greater," Sonia Ortiz-Mercado indicated. "It will have a great impact on persistence rates and completion rates." She is dean of matriculation and early assessment in the California Community College office of the Chancellor.

It is difficult for me to understand how any of this effort will actually help the students who are graduating from high school in a semi-literate state as we know exists today. It feels almost like previous efforts to just pass the kids from grade to grade to get them out and pretend the graduation rates actually mean something in terms of knowledge and ability.

Percentage of Active Students Passing College Preparatory Math by Race/Ethnicity

	African American		Asian		Latino		White	
2002 Courses	# Students	% Pass	# Students	% Pass	# Students	% Pass	# Students	% Pass
Algebra I	175	38	102	88	156	37	85	76
Geometry	173	64	94	92	104	65	78	88
Algebra II	40	63	78	95	53	67	52	91
Elementary Functions	22	82	44	96	20	80	47	96
2003 Courses								
Algebra I	191	49	116	90	179	50	92	87
Geometry	164	75	96	93	106	75	83	91
Algebra II	64	75	82	96	66	80	60	94
Elementary Functions	25	89	56	94	32	85	33	92

2004 Courses	African American		Asian		Latino		White	
	# Students	% Pass	# Students	% Pass	# Students	% Pass	# Students	% Pass
Algebra I	240	62	124	92	192	61	102	90
Geometry	192	68	102	90	122	76	75	90
Algebra II	84	72	94	96	88	71	62	92
Elementary Functions	15	10 0	64	95	45	98	34	93

Index xix

APPENDIX 7:
ACT Provides Tools to Measure College and Career Readiness:

In August 2014, it was reported that nearly a third of high school seniors took the ACT test. With a possible score of 36, California's average composite was 22.3 compared to the national average of 21. Time to cheer? Not really as it relates to the achievement gap.

ACT is a nonprofit in Iowa that provides tools to measure college and career readiness. Fifty-seven percent of the nation's high school seniors took it. Of those taking the test 86% indicated they planned to go to college, but only 69% actually enrolled.

Only 34% of students in California received satisfactory scores in all subject areas. Across the nation the number is even lower at 26%. So things look good for California until you see the results along racial lines. Seventy percent of white students and 65% of Asian students passed. Only 26% of Latinos and 21% of blacks passed.

"High aspirations are wonderful, but in too many cases, students' actual preparation is not aligned with those aspirations," Jon Whitmore, the chief executive of ACT said in a statement. Sadly it is these poor results which is prompting more colleges to ignore the results of ACT tests and return to accepting students based just on their high school grades.

APPENDIX 8:
What Should College Graduates Know?:

An October 2013 survey of recent graduates done and commissioned by the American Council of Trustees and Alumni and conducted by GfK Roper found that barely half knew that the Constitution establishes a separation of powers, 43% failed to identify John Roberts as the Chief Justice, 62% didn't know the correct length of a congressional term in office, and 83% didn't know what the Emancipation Proclamation ordered.

At the high school level, 77% of black students and 67% of Hispanics could not identify that ice is the solid form of water.

Higher education has never been more expensive, or seemingly less demanding. According the 2011 book, *Academically Adrift*, by Richard Arum and Josipa Roksa, full time students in 1961 devoted 40 hours per week to school work and study. By 2003 this had declined to 27 hours. This book goes on to testify that 36% of college graduates had not shown any significant cognitive gains over four years. At issue is whether there are certain books one should read and certain facts one should know to be considered a truly educated person—or at least an educated college graduate.

Perhaps an overwhelming question is not just what to study but learn how to do things and accomplish goals.

APPENDIX 9:
Black Leaders Speak Out:

Black Economist Glen Loury urges poor blacks to stop acting like victims and learn the lessons of civility necessary to make it. "Blacks' problems lie not in the heads of white people but rather in the wasted and completely unfulfilled lives of too many black people."

Former college president Alan Keyes states, "Civil rights leaders have hurt the black underclass by abandoning self-help and economic self-sufficiency effort, preferring legal battles that do not aid the poorest blacks."

Thomas Sowell, economist and senior fellow at the Hoover Institute, *Education, Assumptions vs. History*(1986) stated that In more and more cases, parents of students, with an eye to political exposure, create a more contentious environment in which it is the teacher or the principal who maintains a discreet silence for fear of legal or physical retaliation. The sheer exhaustion of going through 'due process' for every disruptive student who needs to be suspended, is enough to discourage decisive action by many school officials.

The destruction of high-quality black schools has been associated with a breakdown in the basic framework of law and order. "As few as ten percent of the students acting as hard-core troublemakers is enough to make a good education impossible."

John McWhorter, associate professor of linguistics at the University of California at Berkeley, *Losing the Race, Self-Sabotage in Black America*(2001): "At Berkeley, I have found it impossible to avoid nothing less than fearing that a black student in my class is likely to be a problem case. We are trained to say at this point that I am "stereotyping" but I have come to expect this for the simple reason it has been true class after class, year after year. A few white professors I have spoken to reluctantly admit that they have had the same experience over their careers."

Professor McWhorter went on to state that "we must remember that I am writing about UC Berkley – these students are among the best black scholars in the state of California."

APPENDIX 10:
Myths of Achievement Scores:

"Good News from Compton?" (*LA Times*, 21 August 2014) Frederick Traham, a Compton resident and president of the PTA, announced that test scores had risen throughout the district over the past ten years. He also reported a higher graduation rate than in the past.

Traham boasted that Laurel Street Elementary in Compton had experienced "one of the most dramatic jumps in test scores in the entire country." What he does not mention is that ten years ago, the school was predominantly black; today it is 76% Latino and only 22% black. So the real explanation for the increase in achievement may lie in the changing ethnic make-up of the community, something for which school officials hardly deserve credit.

In Santa Ana, California the school district bragged about the great test results for one of its schools in a district that is 92% Latino and with poor academic results historically.

But when we looked into this particular school, Arroyo Elementary School, we found that what made it score so high was the ethnic composition of the pupils which stood at 71% white and 10% Asian. See the chart below:

Arroyo Elementary School

GreatSchools rating: 10 Community rating: API score: 943

K-5 | Public | Santa Ana, CA | Contact info

Groups	Number of Students Included in 2011 Growth API	2011 Growth API	Number of Students Included in 2012 Growth API	2012 Growth API	Number of Students Included in 2013 Growth API	2013 Growth API	Non-Weighted 3-Year Average API*	Weighted 3-Year Average API*
Schoolwide	412	952	412	952	419	944	949	949
Black or African American	4		4		5			
American Indian or Alaska Native	2		1		1			
Asian	33	956	34	969	36	977	967	968
Filipino	3		2		0			
Hispanic or Latino	49	942	45	932	51	919	931	931
Native Hawaiian or Pacific Islander	1		1		0			
White	307	952	311	951	313	944	949	949
Two or More Races	13	997	14	980	13	988	988	988
Socioeconomically Disadvantaged	13	907	9		18	873		
English Learners	7		8		8			
Students with Disabilities	39	920	38	885	44	867	891	890

Student diversity

Index xx

APPENDIX 11:
Mexican Revanchisme (Reclaim the land):

Gilda Ochoa's *Academic Profiling; Latinos, Asian Americans, and the Achievement Gap* (2013) is an in-depth study of a school that is half Hispanic and half Asian. It seeks to explain why Asians do so well in school compared to Hispanics. Aside from the usual views of the family focus, cultural advantage, and other excuses, she makes a rather startling statement on the cause of the gap: "Today, schools persist in English-only policies and Eurocentric curriculum. Such practices are informed by and maintain hierarchies that privilege the English language and dominant values, norms, and expectations. They simultaneously ignore, undermine or outright ridicule the culture and communities of many students."

She goes on to mention Wendy Luttrell's "*Teachers: They All Have Their Pets*" (1993) which remarks that favored students tend to be lighter skinned, more feminine, and middle class. Other students know this, and it fuels resentment and even harassment of "teacher's pets."

APPENDIX 12:
Tax Credit Program in Oklahoma Creates Voucher System:

Martin Friedman, with his wife Rose, established the Friedman Foundation in 1996 to promote his vision of school choice for all children. Starting small at that time it has mushroomed into a major operation and the state now allows tax credits of up to $1,000 per person for contributions of $2,000 or more. For corporations and foundations, the cap is $200,000 which then allows them a $100,000 tax credit.

And with new state action, this gets even better. If a high-income individual promises to give the same amount to the Foundation or any scholarship granting organization (SGO's) for the next three years, he'll generate a 75% tax credit this year followed by a 50% credit in each of the next two years. Thus a $35,000 donation with a promise to do the same for the next two years allows that person to enjoy a reduction of $26,250 the first year and $17,500 for each of the next two.

Students can select any private or parochial school they want to attend. Such a program was approved by the US Supreme Court in Zelman v. Simmons-Harris in 2002.

Public schools have had some fear of this emerging program but their revenue does not vary with enrollment so funding is not impacted even if half the students leave. So it actually increases the amount of funds available to the public schools impacted.

Families of four can enjoy and obtain such scholarships if they earn less than $132,000 per year. It is hoped that as more funds are donated more benefit to the poorest children will flow.

REFERENCE MATERIAL SOURCES

Alexis, Jonas E. *In the Name of Education: How Weird Ideologies Corrupt Our Public Schools, Politics, the Media, Higher Institutions, and History*. N.p.: Xulon Press, 2007.

Baker, John R., *Race.* Oxford Press, London, 1974.
Coulter, Ann, *Mugged.* Sentinel, New York 2012.

Davenport, Patricia, and Gerald Anderson. *Closing the Achievement Gap: No Excuses*. Houston, TX: American Productivity Quality Center Publications, 2002.

D'Souza, Dinesh. *The End of Racism: Principles for a Multiracial Society*. New York: Free Press, 1995.

DuFlour, Richard, Rebecca DuFlour, Robert Eoker, and Gayle Karhanek. *Raising the Bar and Closing the Gap: Whatever It Takes*. Bloomington, IN: Solution Tree Press, 2010.

Entine, Jon. *Taboo: Why Black Athletes Dominate Sports and Why We Are Afraid To Talk About It*. New York: Public Affairs Press, 2000.

Flaherty, Colin, *Don't Make The Black Kids Angry*. Self-Published, 2015.

Goldberg, Bernard. *Bias: A CBS Insider Exposes How the Media Distorts the News*. Washington, DC: Regnery, 2002.

George, W., *Race Heredity and Civilization*. Britain's Publishing, London, 1976.

Herrnstein, Richard J., and Charles Murray. *The Bell Curve: Intelligence and Class Structure in American Life*. New York: Free Press, 1994.

Hirsch, E. D., Jr. *Knowledge Deficit: Closing the Shocking Education Gap for American Children*. Boston: Houghton Mifflin, 2006.

Jensen, Arthur R. *Bias in Mental Testing*. New York: Free Press, 1980.

Lynn, Richard. *Race Differences in Intelligence*. Augusta, GA: Washington Summit Publishers, 2006.

Lynn, Richard, and Tatu Vanhanen. *IQ and Global Inequality*. Augusta, GA: National Policy Institute, 2006.

McWhorter, John. *Losing the Race: Self-Sabotage in Black America*. New York: Free Press, 2000.

Meier, Frank L., *Jensenism, and Skepticism*. Western Press, 2000.

Modgil, Sohan, and Celia Modgil, eds. *Arthur Jensen: Consensus and Controversy*. London: Falman Press, 1987.

Nyberg, Helmuth, *The Scientific Study of General Intelligence*. Paragmon Press 2003.

Nyberg, Helmuth and Jensen, Arthur, *Occupational and Income Related to Psychometrics.* Intelligence Magazine, 1999.

Ochoa, Gilda L. *Academic Profiling: Latinos, Asian Americans, and the Achievement Gap*. Minneapolis: University of Minnesota Press, 2013.

Sowell, Thomas. *Education: Assumptions vs. History*. Stanford, CA: Hoover Institution Press, 1986.

Templeton, Alan R., *Population Genetics and Microevolutionary Theory*. Wiley-Liss, New Jersey, 2006.

UNESCO, *Race and Science.* Columbia University, 1961.

Vernez, Georges, Richard A. Krop, and C. Peter Rydel. *Closing the Education Gap: Benefits and Costs*. Santa Monica, CA: RAND Education, 1999.

Walters, Robert. *As the Pendulum Swings.*: Self-published, 1965.

BIBLIOGRAPHY of ARTHUR R. JENSEN

1955
1. Symonds, P. M., & Jensen, A. R. (1955). A review of six textbooks in educational psychology.
Journal of Educational Psychology, 46, 56-64.

1956
2. Jensen, A. R. (1956). Aggression in fantasy and overt behavior. Unpublished doctoral
dissertation, Columbia University, New York.

1957
3. Jensen, A. R. (1957). Aggression in fantasy and overt behavior. Psychological Monographs, 71, (445), Whole No. 16.
4. Jensen, A. R. (1957). Authoritarian attitudes and personality maladjustment. Journal of
Abnormal and Social Psychology, 54, 303-311.
5. Pope, B., & Jensen, A. R. (1957). The Rorschach as an index of pathological thinking. Journal of Projective Techniques, 21, 59-62.

1958
6. Jensen, A. R. (1958). Personality. Annual Review of Psychology, 9, 295-322.
7. Jensen, A. R. (1958). The Maudsley Personality Inventory. Acta Psychologica, 14, 312-325. (Reprinted in: Savage, R. D.

(Ed.) (1958), Readings in Clinical Psychology. Pergamon Press).
8. Symonds, P. M., & Jensen, A. R. (1958). The predictive significance of fantasy. American Journal of Orthopsychiatry, 28, 73-84.

1959

9. Jensen, A. R. (1959). The reliability of projective techniques: Review of the literature. Acta Psychologica, 16, 3-31.
10. Jensen, A. R. (1959). The reliability of projective techniques: Methodology (pp. 32-67). Amsterdam: North-Holland Publishing Co.
11. Jensen, A. R. (1959). A statistical note on racial differences in the Progressive Matrices. Journal of Consulting Psychology, 23, 272.
12. Jensen, A. R. (1959). Review of the Thematic Apperception Test. In: O. K. Euros (Ed.), Fifth mental measurements yearbook (pp. 310-313). Highland Park, NJ: Gryphon Press.
13. Jensen, A. R. (1959). Review of the Family Relations Test. In: O. K. Euros (Ed.), Fifth mental measurements yearbook (pp. 227-228). Highland Park, NJ: Gryphon Press.
14. Jensen, A. R. (1959). [Review of Perceptual processes and mental illness, by H. J. Eysenck, G. W. Granger, & J. D. Erengelmann.]. Journal of Nervous and Mental Diseases, 128, 469-471.

1960
15. Jensen, A. R. (1960). Holistic personality. [Review of Understanding personalities, by R. Leeper, & R. Leeper, & P. Madison.] Contemporary Psychology, 5, 353-355.
16. Jensen, A. R. (1960). Some criticisms of automated teaching. California Journal of
Instructional Improvement, 3, 32-35.
17. Jensen, A. R. (1960). Teaching machines and individual differences. Automated Teaching Bulletin, 1, 12-16. (Reprinted in: Smith, W. I., & Moore, J. W. (Eds), Programmed learning (pp. 218-226). New York: Van Nostrand, 1962).

1961
18. Jensen, A. R. (1961). On the reformulation of inhibition in Hull's system. Psychological Bulletin, 58, 274-298.
19. Jensen, A. R. (1961). Learning abilities in Mexican-American and Anglo-American children. California Journal of Educational Research, 12, 147-159.
20. Symonds, P. M., & Jensen, A. R. (1961). From adolescent to adult (pp. viii + 413). New York: Columbia University Press.

1962
21. Jensen, A. R. (1962). The von Restorff isolation effect with minimal response learning. Journal of Experimental Psychology, 64, 123-125.
22. Jensen, A. R. (1962). An empirical theory of the serial-position effect. Journal of Psychology, 53, 127-142.
23. Jensen, A. R. (1962). Temporal and spatial effects of serial position. American Journal of Psychology, 75, 390-400.

(Reprinted in: Slamecka, N. J. (Ed.) (1967), Human learning and memory: Selected readings (pp. 117-124). New York: Oxford University Press).
24. Jensen, A. R. (1962). Is the serial position curve invariant? British Journal of Psychology, 53, 159-166.
25. Jensen, A. R. (1962). Transfer between paired-associate and serial learning. Journal of Verbal Learning and Verbal Behavior, 7, 269-280.
26. Jensen, A. R. (1962). Spelling errors and the serial position effect. Journal of Educational Psychology, 53, 105-109. (Reprinted in: Otto, W., & Koenke, K. (Eds) (1969), Readings on corrective and remedial teaching (pp. 346-352). Boston: Houghton-Mifflin; Johnson, R E. (Ed.) (1972), Learning: Theory and practice (pp. 173-179). New York: Crowell).
27. Jensen, A. R. (1962). Extraversion, neuroticism and serial learning. Acta Psychologica, 20, 69-77.
28. Jensen, A. R. (1962). The improvement of educational research. Teachers College Record, 64, 20-27. (Reprinted in: 1963, Education Digest, 28, 18-22; Courtney, E. W. (Ed.) (1965), Applied research in education (pp. 304-316). Totowa, NJ: Littlefield, Adams & Co.).
29. Jensen, A. R. (1962). [Review of Programmed learning: Evolving principles and industrial applications. Foundation for Research on Human Behavior, edited by J. R Lysaught] Contemporary Psychology, 7, 33.
30. Jensen, A. R. (1962). Reinforcement psychology and individual differences. California Journal of Educational Research, 13, 174-178.
31. Jensen, A. R., & Blank, S. S. (1962). Association with ordinal position in serial rote-learning. Canadian Journal of Psychology, 16, 60-63.

32. Jensen, A. R., Collins, C. C, & Vreeland, R. W. (1962). A multiple S-R apparatus for human learning. American Journal of Psychology, 75, 470-476.

1963

33. Jensen, A. R. (1963). Serial rote-learning: Incremental or all-or-none? Quarterly Journal of Experimental Psychology, 15, 27-35.
34. Jensen, A. R. (1963). Learning abilities in retarded, average, and gifted children. MerrillPalmer Quarterly, 9, 123-140. (Reprinted in: DeCecco, J. R (Ed.) (1964), Educational technology: Reading in programmed instruction (pp. 356-375). New York: Holt, Rinehart, and Winston, Inc.).
35. Jensen, A. R. (1963). Learning in the preschool years. Journal of Nursery Education, 18, 133-139. (Reprinted in: Hartup, W. W., & Smothergill, Nancy L. (Eds) (1967), The young child: Reviews of research (pp. 125-135). Washington, D.C.: National Association for the Education of Young Children).
36. Jensen, A. R., & Roden, A. (1963). Memory span and the skewness of the serial-position curve. British Journal of Psychology, 54, 337-349.
37. Jensen, A. R., & Rohwer, W D. Jr. (1963). Verbal mediation in paired-associate and serial learning. Journal of Verbal Learning and Verbal Behavior, 1, 346-352.
38. Jensen, A. R., & Rohwer, W. D. Jr. (1963). The effect of verbal mediation on the learning and retention of paired-associates by retarded adults. American Journal of Mental Deficiency, 68, 80-84.

1964

39. Jensen, A. R. (1964). The Rorschach technique: Are-evaluation. Acta Psychologica, 22, 60-77.
40. Jensen, A. R. (1964). Learning, briefly. [Review of Learning: A survey of psychological interpretations, by W. F. Hill.] Contemporary Psychology, 9, 228-229.

1965

41. Jensen, A. R. (1965). An adjacency effect in free recall. Quarterly Journal of Experimental Psychology, 17, 315-322.
42. Jensen, A. R. (1965). Rote learning in retarded adults and normal children. American Journal of Mental Deficiency, 69, 828-834.
43. Jensen, A. R. (1965). Individual dijferences in learning: Interference factor (pp. 1-160). Cooperative Research Project No. 1867, U.S. Office of Education.
44. Jensen, A. R. (1965). Scoring the Stroop Test. Acta Psychologica, 24, 398-408.
45. Jensen, A. R. (1965). Review of the Maudsley Personality Inventory. In: O. K. Euros (Ed.), Sixth mental measurements yearbook (pp. 288-291). Highland Park, NJ: Gryphon Press.
46. Jensen, A. R. (1965). Review of the Rorschach Test. In: O. K. Euros (Ed.), Sixth mental measurements yearbook (pp. 501-509). Highland Park, NJ: Gryphon Press. (Reprinted in: Eracht, G. H., Hopkins, K., & Stanley, J. C. (Eds) (1972). Perspectives in education and psychological measurement (pp. 292-311). New York: Prentice-Hall).
47. Jensen, A. R. (1965). Review of the make a picture story test. In: O. K. Euros (Ed.), Sixth mental measurements yearbook (pp. 468-470). Highland Park, NJ: Gryphon Press.

48. Jensen, A. R., & Rohwer, W. D. Jr. (1965). Syntactical mediation of serial and pairedassociate learning as a function of age. Child Development, 36, 601-608.
49. Jensen, A. R., & Rohwer, W. D. Jr. (1965). What is learned in serial learning? Journal of Verbal Learning and Verbal Behavior, 4, 62-72. (Reprinted in: Slamecka, N. J. (Ed.) (1967), Human learning and memory (pp. 98-110). New York: Oxford University Press).
50. Eattig, W. P., Allen, M., & Jensen, A. R. (1965). Priority of free recall of newly learned items. Journal of Verbal Learning and Verbal Behavior, 4, 175-179.

1966

51. Jensen, A. R. (1966). The measurement of reactive inhibition in humans. Journal of General Psychology 75, 85-93.
52. Jensen, A. R. (1966). Social class and perceptual learning. Mental Hygiene, 50, 226-239. (Reprinted in: Rogers, Dorothy (Ed.) (1969), Readings in child psychology. New York: Erooks-Cole Publishing Co.).
53. Jensen, A. R. (1966). Individual differences in concept learning. In: H. Klausmeier, & C. Harris (Eds), Analyses of concept learning (pp. 139-154). New York: Merrill, 1966.
(Reprinted in: Eutcher, H. J., & Lomax, L., (1971). Readings in human intelligence (pp. 100- 114). London: Methuen).
54. Jensen, A. R. (1966). Cumulative deficit in compensatory education. Journal of School Psychology, 4, 37-47.
55. Jensen, A. R. (1966). Verbal mediation and educational potential. Psychology in the Schools, 3, 99-109. (Reprinted in: Torrance, E. P, & White, W F. (Eds) (1975), Issues and

advances in educational psychology (2nd ed., pp. 175-188). Ithaca, IL: F. E. Peacock).
56. Jensen, A. R. (1966). Conceptions and misconceptions about verbal mediation. In: M. P. Douglas (Ed.), Claremont Reading Conference (pp. 134-141). Thirtieth Yearbook, Claremont Graduate School.
57. Jensen, A. R. (1966). Intensive, detailed, exhaustive. [Review of Paired-associates learning: The role of meaningfulness, similarity and familiarization, by A. E. Goss & C. F. Nodine.] Contemporary Psychology, 11, 379-380.
58. Jensen, A. R., & Rohwer, W. D. Jr. (1966). The Stroop Color-Word Test: A review. Acta Psychologica, 25, 36-93.

1967
59. Jensen, A. R. (1967). Varieties of individual differences in learning. In: R. M. Gagne (Ed.), Learning and individual differences (pp. 117-135). Columbus, Ohio: Merrill. (Reprinted in: Roweton, W. E. (Ed.) (1972), Humanistic trends in educational psychology. New York: Xerox Co.).
60. Jensen, A. R. (1967). Estimation of the limits of heritabiUty of traits by comparison of monozygotic and dizygotic twins. Science, 75(5, 539. Abstract.
61. Jensen, A. R. (1967). Estimation of the Hmits of heritabiUty of traits by comparison of monozygotic and dizygotic twins. Proceedings of the National Academy of Science, 58, 149-156.
62. Jensen, A. R. (1967). The culturally disadvantaged: Psychological and educational aspects. Educational Research, 10, 4-20.

63. Jensen, A. R. (1967). How much can we boost IQ and scholastic achievement? Proceedings of the California Advisory Council on Educational Research.

1968

64. Jensen, A. R. (1968). Social class, race and genetics: Implications for education. American Educational Research Journal, 5, 1-42. (Reprinted in: Gordon, I. J. (Ed.) (1971). Readings in research in developmental psychology (pp. 54-67). Glenview, IL: Scott, Foresman, & Co.; Clarizio, H. F, Craig, R. C, & Mehrens, W. H. (Eds) (1970). Contemporary issues in educational psychology. New York: AUyn & Bacon).
65. Jensen, A. R. (1968). Patterns of mental ability and socioeconomic status. Science, 160, 439. Abstract.
66. Jensen, A. R. (1968). Patterns of mental ability and socioeconomic status. Proceedings of the National Academy of Sciences, 60, 1330-1337.
67. Jensen, A. R. (1968). Social class and verbal learning. In: M. Deutsch, I. Katz, & A. R. Jensen (Eds), Social class, race, and psychological development (pp. 115-174). New York: Holt, Rinehart, & Winston. (Reprinted in: DeCecco, J. P. (Ed.) (1967). The psychology of language,
thought, and instruction (pp. 103-117). New York: Holt, Rinehart, & Winston).
68. Jensen, A. R. (1968). The culturally disadvantaged and the heredity-environment uncertainty. In: J. Hellmuth (Ed.), Disadvantaged child (Vol. 2, pp. 29-76). Seattle, Washington: Special Child Publications.
69. Jensen, A. R. (1968). Another look at culture-fair testing. In: Western Regional Conference on Testing Problems,

Proceedings for 1968, Measurement for Educational Planning (pp. 50-104). Berkeley, California: Educational Testing Service, Western Office. (Reprinted in: Hellmuth, J. (Ed.), Disadvantaged child (Vol. 3), Compensatory education: A national debate (pp. 53-101). New York: Brunner/Mazel).
70. Jensen, A. R. (1968). Influences of biological, psychological, and social deprivations upon learning and performance. In: Perspectives on human deprivation (pp. 125-137). Washington, D.C.: U.S. Department of Health, Education, and Welfare.
71. Jensen, A. R. (1968). Discussion of Ernst Z. Rothkoph's Two scientific approaches to the management of instruction. In: R. M. Gagne, & W. J. Gephart (Eds), Learning research and school subjects (pp. 134-141). Itasca, IL: F. E. Peacock.
72. Jensen, A. R. (1968). The biology of maladjustment. [Review of Studies of troublesome children, by D. H. Stott.] Contemporary Psychology, 13, 204-206.
73. Jensen, A. R., & Rohwer, W D. Jr. (1968). Mental retardation, mental age, and learning rate. Journal of Educational Psychology, 59, 402^03.
74. Deutsch, M., Katz, I., & Jensen, A. R. (Eds) (1968). Social class, race, and psychological development (pp. v + 423). New York: Holt, Rinehart, & Winston.
75. Lee, S. S., & Jensen, A. R. (1968). Effect of awareness on 3-stage mediated association. Journal of Verbal Learning and Verbal Behavior, 7, 1005-1009.

1969

76. Jensen, A. R. (1969). How much can we boost I. Q. and scholastic achievement? Harvard Educational Review, 39, 1-123. (Reprinted in: Environment, heredity, and intelligence.

Harvard Educational Review, Reprint Series No. 2, 1969 (pp. 1-123); Congressional Record (May 28, 1969, Vol. 115, No. 88, pp. H-4270-4298); Bracht, G. H., Hopkins, K., & Stanley, J. C. (Eds) (1972). Perspectives in educational and psychological measurement (pp. 191-213). New York: Prentice-Hall; Bamette, W. L. Jr. (Ed.) (1976). Readings in psychological tests and measurements (3rd ed., pp. 370-380). Baltimore: Williams & Wilkins).
77. Jensen, A. R. (1969). Reducing the heredity-environment uncertainty. Harvard Educational Review, 39, 449-483. (Reprinted in: Environment, heredity, and intelligence. Harvard Educational Review, Reprint Series No. 2, 1969 (pp. 209-243)).
78. Jensen, A. R. (1969). Intelligence, learning ability, and socioeconomic status. Journal of Special Education, 3, 23-35. (Reprinted in: Mental Health Digest, 1969, 1, 9-12).
79. Jensen, A. R. (1969). Understanding readiness: An occasional paper (pp. 1-17). Urbana, IL: ERIC Clearinghouse on Early Childhood Education, National Laboratory on Early Childhood Education.
80. Jensen, A. R. (1969). Jensen's theory of intelligence: A reply. Journal of Educational
Psychology 60, 427^31.
81. Jensen, A. R. (1969). The promotion of dogmatism. Journal of Social Issues, 25, 212-217; 219-222.
82. Jensen, A. R. (1969). Criticism or propaganda? Am^ncan Psychologist, 24, 1040-1041.
83. Jensen, A. R. (1969). An embattled hypothesis [interview]. Center Magazine, 2, 77-80.

84. Jensen, A. R. (1969). Education ills: Diagnosis and cure? [Review of Who can be educated? by M. Schwebel.] Contemporary Psychology, 14, 362-364.
85. Jensen, A. R. (1969). [Review of Pygmalion in the classroom, by R. Rosenthal & Lenore Jacobson.] American Scientist, 57, 44A-45A.
86. Jensen, A. R. (1969). Race and intelligence: The differences are real. Psychology Today, 3, 4-6. (Reprinted in: Sexton, Patricia C. (Ed.) (1970). Problems and policy in education. New York: AUyn & Bacon; Jacoby, R., & Glauberman, N. (Eds) (1995). The Bell Curve debate: History, documents, opinions. New York: Random House).
87. Rohwer, W D. Jr., & Jensen, A. R. (1969). A reply to Glass. Journal of Educational
Psychology, 60, 417^18.

1970
88. Jensen, A. R. (1970). A theory of primary and secondary familial mental retardation. In: N. R. Ellis (Ed.), International review of research in mental retardation (Vol. 4, pp. 33-105). New York: Academic Press.
89. Jensen, A. R. (1970). Hierarchical theories of mental ability. In: B. Dockrell (Ed.), On
intelligence (pp. 119-190). Toronto: Ontario Institute for Studies in Education.
90. Jensen, A. R. (1970). IQ's of identical twins reared apart. Behavior Genetics, 7, 133-148. (Reprinted in: Eysenck, H. J. (Ed.) (1973). The measurement of intelligence (pp. 273-288). Lancaster, U.K.: Medical and Technical Publishing Co.).
91. Jensen, A. R. (1970). Race and the genetics of inteUigence: A reply to Lewontin. Bulletin of the Atomic

Scientists, 26, 17-23. (Reprinted in: Baer, D. (Ed.) (1973). Heredity and society: Readings in social genetics (pp. 300-311). New York: Macmillan; Block, N. J., & Dworkin, G. (Eds), The IQ controversy (pp. 93-106). New York: Pantheon).

92. Jensen, A. R. (1970). Can we and should we study race differences? In: J. Hellmuth (Ed.), Disadvantaged child (Vol. 3), Compensatory education: A national debate (pp. 124-157). New York: Brunner/Mazel. (Reprinted in: Grigham, J. C, & Weissbach, T. A. (Eds) (1971). Racial attitudes in America: Analysis and findings of social psychology (pp. 401-434). New York: Harper & Row; Journal of the American Anthropological Association, 1971, Anthropological Studies. No. 8.; Wrightsman, L. S., & Brigham, J. C. (Eds) (1973). Contemporary issues in social psychology (2nded., pp. 218-227). Monterey, CA: Brooks/Cole).

93. Jensen, A. R. (1970). Learning ability, intelligence, and educability. In: V. Allen (Ed.), Psychological factors in poverty (pp. 106-132). Chicago: Markham.

94. Jensen, A. R. (1970). The heritability of inteUigence. Science & Engineering, 33, 40-43. (Reprinted in: Saturday Evening Post, Summer, 1972; Rubinstein, J., & Shfe, B. D. (Eds) (1980). Taking Sides: Clashing views on controversial psychological issues (pp. 232-238). Guilford, CN: Dushkin PubHshing Group; Zimbardo, R, & Maslach, C. (Eds) (1973). Psychology for our times: Readings (pp. 129-134). Glenview, IL: Scott, Foresman).

95. Jensen, A. R. (1970). Statement of Dr. Arthur R. Jensen to the General Subcommittee on Education of the Committee on Education and Labor, House of Representatives, 92nd

Congress, second session. Hearings on Emergency School Aid Act of 1970 (pp. 333-342). (H.R. 17846) Washington, D.C.: U.S. Government Printing Office.
96. Jensen, A. R. (1970). [Review of Behavioral genetics: Methods and research, edited by M. Manosevitz, G. Lindzey, and D. D. Thiessen. New York: Appleton-Century-Crofts, 1969.] Social Biology, 17, 151-152.
97. Jensen, A. R. (1970). Parent and teacher attitudes toward integration and busing. Research Resume, No. 43, California Advisory Council on Educational Research, May, 1970.
98. Jensen, A. R. (1970). Selection of minority students in higher education. Toledo Law
Review, Spring-Summer, Nos. 2 & 3, 304^57.
99. Jensen, A. R., & Rohwer, W. D. Jr. (1970). An experimental analysis of learning abilities in culturally disadvantaged children (pp. 1-181). Final Report. Office of Economic Opportunity, Contract No. OEO 2404.

1971

100. Jensen, A. R. (1971). Individual differences in visual and auditory memory. Journal of Educational Psychology, 62, 123-131.
101. Jensen, A. R. (1971). Controversies in intelligence: Heredity and environment. In: D. W. Allen, & E. Seifman (Eds), The teacher's handbook (pp. 642-654). Glenview, IL: Scott, Foresman & Co.
102. Jensen, A. R. (1971). The role of verbal mediation in mental development. Journal of Genetic Psychology, 118, 39-70.

103. Jensen, A. R. (1971). Heredity, environment, and intelligence. In: L. C. Deighton (Ed.), Encyclopedia of education (Vol. 4, pp. 368-380). New York: Macmillan.
104. Jensen, A. R. (1971). The race X sex X ability interaction. In: R. Cancro (Ed.) (1971). Contributions to intelligence (pp. 107-161). New York: Grune & Stratton.
105. Jensen, A. R. (1971). A note on why genetic correlations are not squared. Psychological Bulletin, 75, 223-224.
106. Jensen, A. R. (1971). Hebb's confusion about heritability. American Psychologist, 26, 394-395.
107. Jensen, A. R. (1971). Twin differences and race differences in IQ: A reply to Burgess and Jahoda. Bulletin of the British Psychological Society, 24, 195-198.
108. Jensen, A. R. (1971). Erbhcher I. Q. oder Padagogischer Optimismus vor einem an deren Gericht. Neue Sammlung, 11, 71-76.
109. Jensen, A. R. (1971). Do schools cheat minority children? Educational Research, 14,
3-28.
110. Jensen, A. R. (1971). The phylogeny and ontogeny of intelligence. Perspectives in Biology and Medicine, 15, 37-43.
111. Jensen, A. R. (1971). Heredity and environment: A controversy over IQ and scholastic achievement. In: H. C. Lindgren, & F. Lindgren (Eds), Current readings in educational psychology (2nd ed., pp. 323-327). New York: Wiley.

1972

112. Jensen, A. R. (1972). Genetics and education (pp. vii + 379). London: Methuen (New York: Harper & Row).

113. Jensen, A. R. (1972). A two-factor theory of familial mental retardation. In: J. deGrouchy, F. J. G. Ebling, & I. W. Henderson (Eds) (1972), Human genetics (pp. 263-271). Proceedings of the 4th International Congress of Human Genetics, Paris, September, 1971. Amsterdam: Excerpta Medica.
114. Jensen, A. R. (1972). Review of Analysis of Learning Potential. In: O. K. Euros (Ed.), Seventh mental measurements yearbook (Vol. I, pp. 622-625). Highland Park, NJ: Gryphon Press.
115. Jensen, A. R. (1972). The case for IQ tests: Reply to McClelland. The Humanist, 32, 14.
116. Jensen, A. R. (1972). The causes of twin differences in IQ: A reply to Gage. Phi Delta Kappan, 53,420-421.
117. Jensen, A. R. (1972). Genetics and education: A second look. New Scientist, 56, 96-98.
118. Jensen, A. R. (1972). Scholastic achievement and intelligence (Statement to the U.S. Senate Select Committee on Equal Educational Opportunity). In: Environment, Intelligence, and Scholastic Achievement (pp. 55-68). (A compilation of testimony to the Select Committee on Equal Educational Opportunity, United States Senate, 92nd Congress, 2nd Session, June 1972.) Washington, D.C.: U.S. Government Printing Office, 1972. (Reprinted in: Saturday Evening Post, 1972, 244 (No. 2), 150-152).
119. Jensen, A. R. (1972). Interpretation of heritability. American Psychologist, 27, 973-975.
120. Jensen, A. R. (1972). I.Q. and Race: Ethical issues. The Humanist, 32, 5-6.

121. Jensen, A. R. (1972). Heritability and teachability. In: J. E. Bruno (Ed.), Emerging issues in education (pp. 57-88). Lexington, MA: D. C. Heath.
122. Jensen, A. R. (1972). Comment on De Fries' paper. In: L. Ehrman, G. S. Omenn, & E. Caspari (Eds) (1972), Genetics, environment, and behavior (pp. 23-25). New York: Academic Press.
123. Jensen, A. R. (1972). Discussion of Tobach's paper. In: Lee Ehrman, G. S. Omenn, & E. Caspari (Eds) (1972). Genetics, environment, and behavior (pp. 240-246). New York: Academic Press.
124. Jensen, A. R. (1972). Educabilite, transmission hereditaire et differences entre populations. (Educability, heritability, and population differences.) Revue de Psychologie Appliquee, 22, 21-34.
125. Jensen, A. R. (1972). [Review of Race, culture and intelligence, edited by K. Richardson, D. Spears, & M. Richards (Middlesex, England: Penguin, 1972).] New Society, 491, 408-410.
126. Jensen, A. R. (1972). Sir Cyril Burt [Obituary]. Psychometrika, 37, 115-117.
127. Jensen, A. R. (1972). Jensen on Hirsch on "jensenism". Educational Researcher, 1, 15-16.
128. Jensen, A. R. (1972). Assessment of racial desegregation in the Berkeley Schools. In: D. Adelson (Ed.), Man as the measure: The crossroads (pp. 116-133). (Community Psychology Series, No. 1. American Psychological Association, Div. 27). New York: Behavioral Publications, Inc.

129. Jensen, A. R. (1972). Educability, heritability, and population differences. Proceedings of the 17th International Congress of Applied Psychology. Brussels, Belgium: Editest.
130. Jensen, A. R. (1972). Letter-to-the-Editor [on genetic IQ differences among social classes]. Perspectives in Biology and Medicine, 116, 154-156.
131. Jensen, A. R. (1972). Review of WLW Culture Fair Inventory. In: O. K. Buros (Ed.), Seventh mental measurements yearbook (Vol. 1, pp. 720-721). Highland Park, NJ: Gryphon Press.
132. Jensen, A. R. (1972). The IQ controversy: A reply to Layzer. Cognition, 4, 427-452.
133. Jensen, A. R. (1972). Empirical basis of the periodic table of human cultures. In: E. Haskell (Ed.) (1972), Full circle: The moral force of unified science (pp. 156-164). New York: Gordon & Breach.

1973
134. Jensen, A. R. (1973). A case for dysgenics. The Journal: Forum for Contemporary History, 2 (4), 1-6.
135. Jensen, A. R. (1973). Some facts about the IQ. The Journal: Forum for Contemporary History, 2 (7), 6-8.
136. Jensen, A. R. (1973). Expanding the thesis: The IQ controversy. [Review of IQ in the meritocracy, by R. J. Hermstein. Boston: Little-Brown, 1973.]. Book World, Chicago
Tribune, June 24, 1973.
137. Jensen, A. R. (1973). On "Jensenism": A reply to critics. In: B. Johnston (Ed.), Education yearbook, 1973-74 (pp. 276-298). New York: Macmillan Educational Corporation.

138. Jensen, A. R. (197^. Race, intelligence and genetics: The differences are real. Psychology Today, 7, 80-86. (kepj^nted in: Durland, W. R., & Bruening, W. H. (Eds) (1975). Ethical issues (pp. 403-414). Palo Alto, CA: Mayfield; Whitehead, Joan M. (Ed.) (1975). Personality and learning 1 (pp. 345-351). London: Hodder & Stroughton; Schell, R. E. (Ed.) (1977). Readings in developmental psychology Today (pp. 230-234), (2nd ed.). New York: Random House; Brigham, J. C, & Wrightsman, L. S. (Eds) (1977). Contemporary issues in social psychology (3rd ed.). Monterey, CA: Brooks/Cole).
139. Jensen, A. R. (1973). Critics of the IQ. [Review of The fallacy of IQ, edited by C. Senna.
New York: The Third Press, 1973]. The Georgia Review, 27, 439-445.
140. Jensen, A. R. (1973). Personality and scholastic achievement in three ethnic groups. British Journal of Educational Psychology, 43, 115-125.
141. Jensen, A. R. (1973). Let's understand Skodak and Skeels, finally. Educational
Psychologist, 10, 30-35.
142. Jensen, A. R. (1973). Skinner and human differences. In: H. Wheeler (Ed.), Beyond the punitive society (pp. 117-198). San Francisco: W. H. Freeman.
143. Jensen, A. R. (1973). Educability and group differences (pp. xiii + 407). London: Methuen (New York: Harper & Row).
144. Jensen, A. R. (1973). Educational differences (pp. xiii + 462). London: Methuen. (New York: Barnes & Noble).
145. Jensen, A. R. (1973). Bildungsfahigkeit, Erblichkeit und Bevolkerungsunterschiede. Neue Anthropologic, 1, 37-43.

146. Jensen, A. R. (1973). Level I and Level II abilities in three ethnic groups. American
Educational Research Journal, 4, 263-276.
147. Jensen, A. R. (1973). Wie sehr konnen wir Intelligenz ^Quotient und scheinlische Leistung steigert? In: H. Skowronek (Ed.) (1973), Umwelt und Begabung. Stuttgart, W. Germany: KlettCotta. (Paperback edition published by Ullstein Taschenbuch Verlag, 1982).
148. Jensen, A. R., & Frederiksen, J. (1973). Free recall of categorized and uncategorized lists: A test of the Jensen hypothesis. Journal of Educational Psychology, 65, 304-312.

1974

149. Jensen, A. R. (1974). What is the question? What is the evidence? [Autobiography]. In: T. S. Krawiec (Ed.) (1974), The psychologists (Vol. 2, pp. 203-244). New York: Oxford University Press.
150. Jensen, A. R. (1974). Kinship correlations reported by Sir Cyril Burt. Behavior Genetics, 4 (1), 1-28.
151. Jensen, A. R. (1974). [Review of Abilities: Their structure, growth, and action, by R. B. Cattell. Boston: Houghton-Mifflin, 1971.] American Journal of Psychology, 87, 290-296.
152. Jensen, A. R. (1974). [Review of Genetic diversity and human equality, by Th. Dobzhansky.
New York: Basic Books, 1973.]. Perspectives in Biology and Medicine, 17, 430-434.
153. Jensen, A. R. (1974). How biased are culture-loaded tests? Genetic Psychology
Monographs, 90, 185-244.

154. Jensen, A. R. (1974). Effects of race of examiner on the mental test scores of white and black pupils. Journal of Educational Measurement, 11, 1-14.
155. Jensen, A. R. (1974). Ethnicity and scholastic achievement. Psychological Reports, 34, 659-668.
156. Jensen, A. R. (1974). Cumulative deficit: A testable hypothesis? Developmental Psychology, 10, 996-1019.
157. Jensen, A. R. (1974). Interaction of Level I and Level II abilities with race and
socioeconomic status. Journal of Educational Psychology, 66, 99-111. (Reprinted in:
Wittrock, M. C. (Ed.) (1972). Learning and instruction (pp. 270-290). Berkeley, CA:
McCutchan).
158. Jensen, A. R. (1974). Equality for minorities. In: H. J. Walberg (Ed.), Evaluating
educational performance (pp. 175-222). Berkeley, CA: McCutchan.
159. Jensen, A. R. (1974). The strange case of Dr. Jensen and Mr. Hydel American Psychologist, 29, 467-468.
160. Jensen, A. R. (1974). Educability and group differences. Nature, 250, 713-714.
161. Jensen, A. R. (1974). Race and intelligence: The case for genetics. The Times Educational Supplement, London, September 20, 1974, No. 3095, 20-21.

1975

162. Jensen, A. R. (1975). The price of inequality. Oxford Review of Education, 1 (1), 13-25.

163. Jensen, A. R. (1975). Les fondements scientifiques des inegalites ethniques. Le Monde Diplomatique, June 1975, No. 255, 19.
164. Jensen, A. R. (1975). A theoretical note on sex linkage and race differences in spatial ability. Behavior Genetics, 5, 151-164.
165. Jensen, A. R. (1975). The meaning of heritability in the behavioral sciences. Educational Psychologist, 11, 171-183.
166. Jensen, A. R. (1975). Panorama of modem behavioral genetics. [Review of Introduction to behavioral genetics, by G. E. McCleam & J. C. DeFries. San Francisco: Freeman, 1973]. Contemporary Psychology, 20, 926-928.
167. Jensen, A. R. (1975). Race and mental ability. In: J. F. Ebling (Ed.), Racial variation in man (pp. 71-108). London: Institute of Biology/Blackwell.
168. Jensen, A. R. (1975). Gibt es Unterschiede zwischen Schwarzen und Weissen? Psychologic Heute, Jan. 1975, 63-75.
169. Jensen, A. R. (1975). Interview: Rasse und Begabung. Nation Europa, September 1975, 19-28.
170. Jensen, A. R., & Figueroa, R. A. (1975). Forward and backward digit span interaction with race and IQ: Predictions from Jensen's theory. Journal of Educational Psychology, 67, 882-893.

1976

171. Jensen, A. R. (1976). Race differences, strategy training, and improper inference. Journal of Educational Psychology, 68, 130-131.
172. Jensen, A. R. (1976). Equality and diversity in education. In: N. F. AshUne, T. R. PezuUo, & C. I. Norris (Eds) (1976),

Education, inequality, and national policy (pp. 125-136). Lexington, MA: Lexington Books.
173. Jensen, A. R. (1976). Addendum to human diversity discussion. In: B. D. Davis, & R Flaherty (Eds) (1976), Human diversity: Its causes and social significance (pp. 223-228). Cambridge, MA: Ballinger.
174. Jensen, A. R. (1976). Twins' IQ's: A reply to Schwartz and Schwartz. Behavior Genetics, 6, 369-371.
175. Jensen, A. R. (1976). Eine Zweifactorentheorie des familidren Schwachsinns. Neue
Anthropologic, 4, 53-60.
176. Jensen, A. R. (1976). Test bias and construct vaHdity. Phi Delta Kappan, 58, 34-346.
177. Jensen, A. R. (1976). Heritability of IQ [Letter-to-the-Editor]. Science, 194, 6-14.
178. Jensen, A. R. (1976). The problem of genotype-environment correlation in the estimation of heritability from monozygotic and dizygotic twins. Acta Geneticae Medicae et Gemellologiae, 25, 86-99.

1977
179. Jensen, A. R. (1977). An examination of culture bias in the Wonderlic Personnel Test. Intelligence, 1, 51-64.
180. Jensen, A. R. (1977). Cumulative deficit in IQ of blacks in the rural South. Developmental Psychology, 13, 1841 91. (Reprinted in: Willerman, L., & Turner, R. G. (Eds) (1979), Readings about individual and group differences (pp. 83-91). San Francisco: W. H. Freeman).
181. Jensen, A. R. (1977). Race and mental ability. In: A. H. Halsey (Ed.), Heredity and
environment (pp. 215-262). London: Methuen.

182. Jensen, A. R. (1977). An unfounded conclusion in M. W. Smith's analysis of culture bias in the Stanford-Binet intelligence scale. Genetic Psychology Monographs, 130, 113-115.
183. Jensen, A. R. (1977). Did Sir Cyril Burt fake his research on heritability of intelligence? Phi Delta Kappan, 58, 471^92. (Reprinted in: Education Digest, March, 1977, 42, 43-45).
184. Jensen, A. R. (1977). Die falschen Anschultdigungen gegen Sir Cyril Burt. Neue
Anthropologic, 5, 15-16.

1978

185. Jensen, A. R. (1978). Genetic and behavioral effects of nonrandom mating. In: R. T.
Osborne, C. E. Noble, & N. Weyl (Eds), Human variation (pp. 51-105). New York:
Academic Press.
186. Jensen, A. R. (1978). Sex linkage and race differences in spatial ability: A reply. Behavioral Genetics, 8, 213-217.
187. Jensen, A. R. (1978). Sir Cyril Burt in perspective. American Psychologist, 33, 499-503.
188. Jensen, A. R. (1978). The current status of the IQ controversy. Australian Psychologist, 13, 7-28.
189. Jensen, A. R. (1978). The nature of intelligence and its relation to learning. In: S. MurraySmith (Ed.), Melbourne studies in education (pp. 107-133). Melbourne University Press. (Reprinted in: Journal of Research and Development in Education, 12, 79-95).
190. Jensen, A. R. (1978). Racism refuted [Correspondence]. Nature, 274, 738.

191. Jensen, A. R. (1978). Zum Stand des Streits um die Intelligenz. Neue Anthropologic, 6, 29-40.
192. Jensen, A. R. (1978). IQ controversy. Baltimore Sun, Nov. 24, 1978, p. A12.
193. Jensen, A. R. (1978). Citation Classics (How much can we boost IQ and scholastic
achievement?). Current Contents, No. 41, (October 9), 16.

1979
194. Jensen, A. R. (1979). g: Outmoded theory or unconquered frontier? Creative Science and Technology, 2, 16-29.
195. Jensen, A. R. (1979). [Review of Inheritance of creative intelligence, by J. L. Karlsson. Chicago: Nelson-Hall, 1978.] Journal of Nervous and Mental Diseases, 167, 711-713.
196. Jensen, A. R., & Marisi, D. Q. (1979). A note on the heritability of memory span. Behavior Genetics, 9, 379-387.
197. Jensen, A. R., & Munro, E. (1979). Reaction time, movement time, and intelligence.
Intelligence, 3, 121-126.
198. Jensen, A. R., & Osborne, R. T. (1979). Forward and backward digit span interaction with race and IQ: A longitudinal developmental comparison. Indian Journal of Psychology, 54, 75-87.

1980
199. Jensen, A. R. (1980). Bias in mental testing (pp. xiii + 786). New York: The Free Press (London: Methuen).
200. Jensen, A. R. (1980). Uses of sibling data in educational and psychological research.
American Educational Research Journal, 17, 153-170.

201. Jensen, A. R. (1980). Chronometric analysis of intelligence. Journal of Social and
Biological Structures, 3, 103-122.
202. Jensen, A. R. (1980). Precis of Bias in Mental Testing. Behavioral and Brain Sciences, 3, 325-333.
203. Jensen, A. R. (1980). Correcting the bias against mental testing: A preponderance of peer agreement. Behavioral and Brain Sciences, 3, 359-371.
204. Jensen, A. R. (1980). A critical look at test bias: Fallacies and manifestations. New
Horizons, 21, 44-64.
205. Jensen, A. R., & Inouye, A. R. (1980). Level I and Level II abilities in Asian, White, and Black children. Intelligence, 4, 41-49.

1981

206. Jensen, A. R. (1981). Straight talk about mental tests (pp. xiv + 269). New York: The Free Press.
207. Jensen, A. R. (1981). Raising the IQ: The Ramey and Haskins Study. Intelligence, 5,
29-40.
208. Jensen, A. R. (1981). Obstacles, problems, and pitfalls in differential psychology. In: S. Scan* (Ed.), Race, social class, and individual differences in IQ (pp. 483-514). Hillsdale, NJ: Erlbaum.
209. Jensen, A. R. (1981). Reaction time and inteUigence. In: M. Friedman, J. P. Das, & N. O'Connor (Eds), Intelligence and learning (pp. 39-50). New York: Plenum.
210. Jensen, A. R. (1981). Impressions of India. Update (Graduate School of Education,
University of California, Berkeley), Winter.

211. Jensen, A. R. (1981). Citation Classic (The Stroop color-word test: A review). Current Contents, 13, 20.
212. Jensen, A. R. (1981). An interview with Arthur Jensen. Communique (National Association of School Psychologists), 10, 3-5.
213. Jensen, A. R. (1981). Taboo, constraint, and responsibility in educational research. New Horizons, 22, 11-20.
214. Jensen, A. R. (1981). A nontechnical guide to the IQ controversy. New Horizons, 22, 21-26.
215. Jensen, A. R., Schafer, E. W. R, & Crinella, E (1981). Reaction time, evoked brain
potentials, and psychometric g in the severely retarded. Intelligence, 5, 179-197.

1982

216. Jensen, A. R. (1982). Intelligence. In: S. B. Parker (Ed.), Encyclopedia of science and technology (5th ed.). New York: McGraw-Hill.
217. Jensen, A. R. (1982). Bias in mental testing: A final word. Behavioral and Brain Sciences, 5, 339-340.
218. Jensen, A. R. (1982). The chronometry of intelligence. In: R. J. Sternberg (Ed.), Advances in the psychology of human intelligence (Vol. 1, pp. 255-310). Hillsdale, NJ: Erlbaum.
219. Jensen, A. R. (1982). Reaction time and psychometric g. In: H. J. Eysenck (Ed.), A model for intelligence (pp. 93-132). New York: Springer.
220. Jensen, A. R. (1982). Changing conceptions of intelligence. Education and Training of the Mentally Retarded, 17, 3-5.

221. Jensen, A. R. (1982). The debunking of scientific fossils and straw persons. [An essayreview of The mismeasure of man, by S. J. Gould.]. Contemporary Education Review, 1, 121-135.
222. Jensen, A. R. (1982). Level I/Level II: Factors or categories? Journal of Educational
Psychology, 74, 868-873.
223. Jensen, A. R. (1982). The race concept: Physical variation and correlated socially significant behavioral variation. Current Anthropology, 23, 649-650.
224. Jensen, A. R., & Reynolds, C. R. (1982). Race, social class, and ability patterns on the WISC-R. Personality and Individual Differences, 3, 423-438.

1983

225. Jensen, A. R. (1983). Sir Cyril Burt: A personal recollection. Association of Educational Psychologists Journal, 6, 13-20.
226. Jensen, A. R. (1983). Effects of inbreeding on mental-ability factors. Personality and
Individual Dijferences, 4, 71-87.
227. Jensen, A. R. (1983). The nonmanipulable and effectively manipulable variables in
education. Education and Society, 51-62. (Reprinted in: New Horizons, 1983, 24, 31-50).
228. Jensen, A. R. (1983). [Review of The testing of Negro intelligence (Vol. II), edited by R. T. Osborne, & F. C. J. McGurk.] Personality and Individual Dijferences, 4, 234-235.
229. Jensen, A. R. (1983). [Review of The inheritance of personality and ability, by R. B.
Cattell.] Personality and Individual Dijferences, 4, 365-368.

230. Jensen, A. R. (1983). The definition of intelligence and factor score indeterminacy. The Behavioral and Brain Sciences, 6, 313-315.
231. Jensen, A. R. (1983). Again, how much can we boost IQ? [Review of How and how much can intelligence be increased, edited by D. K. Detterman & R. J. Sternberg.] Contemporary Psychology, 28, 756-758.
232. Jensen, A. R. (1983). Critical flicker frequency and intelligence. Intelligence, 7, 217-225.
233. Jensen, A. R. (1983). Taboo, constraint, and responsibility in educational research. Journal of Social, Political and Economic Studies, 8, 301-311.
234. Jensen, A. R. (1983). Beyond Groth's sociological criticism of psychometrics. Wisconsin Sociologist, 20, 102-105.
235. Jensen, A. R., & Reynolds, C. R. (1983). Sex differences on the WISC-R. Personality and Individual Differences, 4, 223-226.
236. Reynolds, C. R., & Jensen, A. R. (1983). WISC-R subscale patterns of abilities of blacks and whites matched on full scale IQ. Journal of Educational Psychology, 75, 207-214.
237. Sen, A., Jensen, A. R., Sen, A. K., & Arora, I. (1983). Correlation between reaction time and intelligence in psychometrically similar groups in America and India. Applied Research in Mental Retardation, 4, 139-152.

1984

238. Jensen, A. R. (1984). Francis Galton (1822-1911). In: R. J. Corsini (Ed.), Encyclopedia of psychology (Vol. 2, p. 43). New York: Wiley.

239. Jensen, A. R. (1984). Karl Pearson (1857-1936). In: R. J. Corsini (Ed.), Encyclopedia of psychology (Vol. 2, pp. 490-491). New York: Wiley.
240. Jensen, A. R. (1984). Charles Edward Spearman (1863-1945). In: R. J. Corsini (Ed.), Encyclopedia of psychology (Vol. 3, pp. 353-354). New York: Wiley.
241. Jensen, A. R. (1984). Louis Leon Thurstone (1887-1955). In: R. J. Corsini (Ed.),
Encyclopedia of psychology (Vol. 3, pp. 426-427). New York: Wiley.
242. Jensen, A. R. (1984). Law of filial regression. In: R. J. Corsini (Ed.), Encyclopedia of psychology (Vol. 2, pp. 280-281). New York: Wiley.
243. Jensen, A. R. (1984). Cultural bias in tests. In: R. J. Corsini (Ed.), Encyclopedia of
psychology (Vol. 1, pp. 331-332). New York: Wiley.
244. Jensen, A. R. (1984). Inbreeding in human factors. In: R. J. Corsini (Ed.), Encyclopedia of psychology (Vol. 2, pp. 191-192). New York: Wiley.
245. Jensen, A. R. (1984). General intelligence factor. In: R. J. Corsini (Ed.), Encyclopedia of psychology (Vol. 2, p. 48). New York: Wiley.
246. Jensen, A. R. (1984). Heritability. In: R. J. Corsini (Ed.), Encyclopedia of psychology (Vol. 2, p. 108). New York: Wiley.
247. Jensen, A. R. (1984). Test bias: Concepts and criticisms. In: C. R. Reynolds, & R. T. Brown (Eds) (1984), Perspectives on bias in mental testing (pp. 507-586). New York: Plenum.
248. Jensen, A. R. (1984). Political ideologies and educational research. Phi Delta Kappan, 65, 460-462.

249. Jensen, A. R. (1984). The limited plasticity of human inteUigence. New Horizons, 25, 18-22.
250. Jensen, A. R. (1984). Mental speed and levels of analysis. The Behavioral and Brain
Sciences, 7, 295-296.
251. Jensen, A. R. (1984). Test validity: g versus the specificity doctrine. Journal of Social and Biological Structures, 7, 93-118.
252. Jensen, A. R. (1984). Jensen oversimplified: A reply to Sternberg. Journal of Social and Biological Structures, 7, 127-130.
253. Jensen, A. R. (1984). [Review of Intelligence and national achievement, edited by R. B. Cattell.] Personality and Individual Differences, 5, 491-492.
254. Jensen, A. R. (1984). Sociobiology and differential psychology: The arduous chmb from plausibility to proof. In: J. R. Royce, & L. P. Mos (Eds), Annals of theoretical psychology (Vol. 2, pp. 49-58). New York: Plenum.
255. Jensen, A. R. (1984). Constraint and responsibility in educational research. Journal of Social, Political and Economic Studies. * side mangier.
256. Jensen, A. R. (1984). The black-white difference on the K-ABC: Implications for future tests. Journal of Special Education, 18, 377-408.
257. Jensen, A. R. (1984). Objectivity and the genetics of IQ: A reply to Steven Selden. Phi Delta Kappan, 66, 284-286.
258. Agrawal, N., Sinha, S. N., & Jensen, A. R. (1984). Effects of inbreeding on Raven Matrices. Behavior Genetics, 14, 579-585.
259. Vernon, R A., & Jensen, A. R. (1984). Individual and group differences in intelligence and speed of information

processing. Personality and Individual Differences, 5, 41 \-A2?>.

1985

260. Jensen, A. R. (1985). Compensatory education and the theory of intelligence. Phi Delta Kappan, 66, 554-558. (Reprinted in: Slife, B. (Ed.), Taking sides: Clashing views on controversial issues (8th ed.). Guilford, CT: Dushkin).
261. Jensen, A. R. (1985). Armed Services Vocational Aptitude Battery. Measurement and Evaluation in Counseling and Development, 18, 32-37.
262. Jensen, A. R. (1985). Review of the Predictive AbiUty Test, Adult Edition. In: J. V Mitchell, Jr. (Ed.), The ninth mental measurements yearbook (Vol. 2, pp. 1184-1185). Lincoln, NE: University of Nebraska Press.
263. Jensen, A. R. (1985). Review of Minnesota Spatial Relations Test, Revised Edition. In: J. V. Mitchell, Jr. (Ed.), The ninth mental measurements yearbook (Vol. 2, pp. 1014-1015). Lincoln, NE: University of Nebraska Press.
264. Jensen, A. R. (1985). Methodological and statistical techniques for the chronometric study of mental abilities. In: C. R. Reynolds, & V. L. Willson (Eds), Methodological and statistical advances in the study of individual differences (pp. 51-116). New York: Plenum.
265. Jensen, A. R. (1985). Race differences and Type II errors: A comment on Borkowski and KJrause. Intelligence, 9, 33-39.
266. Jensen, A. R. (1985). The nature of the black-white difference on various psychometric tests: Spearman's hypothesis. The Behavioral and Brain Sciences, 8, 193-219.

267. Jensen, A. R. (1985). The black-white difference in g: A phenomenon in search of a theory. The Behavioral and Brain Sciences, 8, 246-263.
268. Jensen, A. R. (1985). Humphrey's attenuated test of Spearman's hypothesis. Intelligence, 9, 285-289.
269. Jensen, A. R. (1985). Immunoreactive theory and the genetics of mental ability. The
Behavioral and Brain Sciences, 8, 453.
270. Cohn, S. J., Carlson, J. S., & Jensen, A. R. (1985). Speed of information processing in academically gifted youths. Personality and Individual Differences, 6, 621-629.

1986

271. Jensen, A. R. (1986). Intelligence: "Definition," measurement, and future research. In: R. J. Sternberg, & D. K. Detterman (Eds), What is intelligence? Contemporary viewpoints on its nature and definition. Norwood, NJ: Ablex.
272. Jensen, A. R. (1986). The theory of inteUigence. In: S. Modgil, & C. Modgil (Eds), Hans Eysenck: Searching for a scientific basis for human behavior. London: Palmer Press.
273. Jensen, A. R. (1986). g: Artifact or reality? Journal of Vocational Behavior, 29, 301-331.
274. Jensen, A. R. (1986). [Review of Academic work and educational excellence: Raising student productivity, edited by T. M. Tomlinson & H. J. Walberg.] Educational Evaluation and Policy Analysis, 8, 447-451.
275. Jensen, A. R., & Vernon, R A. (1986). Jensen's reaction time studies: A reply to Longstreth. Intelligence, 10, 153-179.

1987

276. Jensen, A. R. (1987). Citation Classic: (Educability and group differences). Current
Contents: Social & Behavioral Sciences, 19 (46).
277. Jensen, A. R. (1987). Citation Classic: (Bias in mental testing). Current Contents: Social & Behavioral Sciences, 19 (46).
278. Jensen, A. R. (1987). Process differences and individual differences in some cognitive tasks. Intelligence, 11, 107-136.
279. Jensen, A. R. (1987). Unconfounding genetic and nonshared environmental effects. The Behavioral and Brain Sciences, 10, 26-27.
280. Jensen, A. R. (1987). The plasticity of "inteUigence" at different levels of analysis. In: J. Lochhead, J. Bishop, & D. Perkins (Eds), Thinking: Progress in research and teaching. Philadelphia: Franklin Institute Press.
281. Jensen, A. R. (1987). Individual differences in mental ability. In: J. A. Glover, & R. R. Ronning (Eds), A history of educational psychology. New York, Plenum.
282. Jensen, A. R. (1987). The g beyond factor analysis. In: R. R. Ronning, J. A. Glover, J. C. Conoley, & J. C. Witt (Eds), The influence of cognitive psychology on testing (pp. 87-142). Hillsdale, NJ: Erlbaum.
283. Jensen, A. R. (1987). Differential psychology: Towards consensus. In: M. Modgil, & C. Modgil (Eds), Arthur Jensen: Consensus and controversy. London: Palmer Press, Ltd.
284. Jensen, A. R. (1987). ^ as a focus of concerted research effort [Editorial]. Intelligence, 11, 193-198.
285. Jensen, A. R. (1987). Intelligence as a fact of nature. Zeitschrift fUr Pddagogische
Psychologie, 1, 157-169.

286. Jensen, A. R. (1987). Individual differences in the Hick paradigm. In: P. A. Vernon (Ed.), Speed of information processing and intelligence. Norwood, NJ: Ablex.
287. Jensen, A. R. (1987). Mental chronometry in the study of learning disabilities. Mental
Retardation and Learning Disability Bulletin, 15, 67-88.
288. Jensen, A. R. (1987). Further evidence for Spearman's hypothesis concerning black-white differences on psychometric tests. The Behavioral and Brain Sciences, 10, 512-519.
289. Jensen, A. R., & McGurk, F. C. J. (1987). Black-white bias in "cultural" and "noncultural" test items. Personality and Individual Differences, 8, 295-301.
290. Naglieri, J. A., & Jensen, A. R. (1987). Comparison of black-white differences on the WISC-R and the K-ABC: Spearman's hypothesis. Intelligence, 11, 21-43.

1988

291. Jensen, A. R. (1988). Mongoloid mental ability: Evolution or culture? Mensa Research Bulletin, 24, 23-25.
292. Jensen, A. R. (1988). [Review of Practical intelligence: Nature and origins of competence in the everyday world, edited by R. J. Sternberg & R. K. Wagner.] Personality and Individual Differences, 9, 199-200.
293. Jensen, A. R. (1988). Speed of information processing and population differences. In: S. H. Irvine (Ed.), The cultural context of human ability. London: Cambridge University Press.
294. Jensen, A. R. (1988). Review of the Armed Services Vocational Aptitude Battery. In: J. T. Kopes & M. M. Mastie

(Eds), A counselor's guide to vocational guidance instruments. The National Vocational Guidance Association.
295. Jensen, A. R. (1988). Sex differences in arithmetic computation and reasoning in
prepubertal boys and girls. Behavioral and Brain Sciences, 77, 198-199.
296. Jensen, A. R., & Faulstich, M. E. (1988). Psychometric g in black and white prisoners. Personality and Individual Differences, 9, 925-928.
297. Jensen, A. R., Larson, J., & Paul, S. M. (1988). Psychometric g and mental processing speed on a semantic verification test. Personality and Individual Differences, 9, 243-255.
298. Jensen, A. R., Saccuzzo, D. P., & Larson, G. E. (1988). Equating the Standard and Advanced Forms of the Raven Progressive Matrices. Educational and Psychological Measurement, 48, 1091-1095.
299. Cohn, S. J., Cohn, C. M. G., & Jensen, A. R. (1988). Myopia and inteUigence: A pleiotropic relationship? Human Genetics, 80, 53-58.
300. Kranzler, J. H., Whang, P. A., & Jensen, A. R. (1988). Jensen's use of the Hick paradigm: Visual attention and order effects. Intelligence, 12, 371-391.

1989

301. Jensen, A. R. (1989). The relationship between learning and intelligence. Learning and Individual Differences, 1, 37-62.
302. Jensen, A. R. (1989). Phihp Ewart Vernon (1905-1987) [Obituary]. Psychologist, 44, 844.

303. Jensen, A. R. (1989). "Revised" Updated. [Review of Intelligence: Its structure, growth and action, by R. B. Cattell.] Contemporary Psychology, 34, 140-141.
304. Jensen, A. R. (1989). Raising IQ without increasing gl A review of "The Milwaukee
Project: Preventing mental retardation in children at risk." Developmental Review, 9,
234-258.
305. Jensen, A. R. (1989). "Total perceived value" as the basis of assortative mating in humans. The Behavioral and Brain Sciences, 12, 531.
306. Jensen, A. R. (1989). New findings on the intellectually gifted. New Horizons, 30, 73-80.
307. Jensen, A. R., Cohn, S. J., & Cohn, C. M. G. (1989). Speed of information processing in academically gifted youths and their siblings. Personality and Individual Differences, 10, 29-34.
308. Buckhalt, J., & Jensen, A. R. (1989). The British Ability Scales Speed of Information
Processing subtest: What does it measure? British Journal of Educational Psychology, 59,
100-107.
309. Kranzler, J. H., & Jensen, A. R. (1989). Inspection time and intelligence: A meta-analysis. Intelligence, 13, 329-347.
310. Reed, T. E., & Jensen, A. R. (1989). Short latency visual evoked potentials (VEPs), visual tract speed, and intelligence. Significant correlations. Abstract. Behavior Genetics, 19, 772-773.

1990
311. Jensen, A. R. (1990). Speed of information processing in a calculating prodigy. Intelligence, 14, 259-274.
312. Jensen, A. R. (1990). Straight history. [Review of Schools as sorters: Lewis M. Terman, applied psychology, and the intelligence testing movement, 1890-1930, by R D. Chapman.] Contemporary Psychology, 35, 1147-1148.
313. Jensen, A. R., & Reed, T. E. (1990). Simple reaction time as a suppressor variable in the chronometric study of intelligence. Intelligence, 14, 375-388.

1991
314. Jensen, A. R. (1991). Spearman's g and the problem of educational equality. Oxford Review of Education, 17(2), 169-187.
315. Jensen, A. R. (1991). General mental ability: From psychometrics to biology. Psychodiagnostique, 16, 134-144.
316. Jensen, A. R. (1991). Speed of cognitive processes: A chronometric anchor for
psychometric tests of g. Psychological Test Bulletin, 4, 59-70.
317. Jensen, A. R. (1991). IQ and Science: The mysterious Burt affair. The Public Interest. No. 105, 93-106.
318. Jensen, A. R. (1991). Review of G. E. Thomas (Ed.), ""U.S. race relations in the 1980s and 1990s: Challenges and alternatives" (New York: Hemisphere Publishing Corporation.) Personality and Individual Differences, 12, 321-322.
319. Jensen, A. R. (1991). Spirmanov g factor: Veze izmedu psihometrije i biologije. Psihologija, 24, 167-193.

320. Kranzler, J. H., & Jensen, A. R. (1991). The nature of psychometric g: Unitary process or a number of independent processes? Intelligence, 15, 391-A22.
321. Kranzler, J. H., & Jensen, A. R. (1991). Unitary g: Unquestioned postulate or empirical fact? Intelligence, 15, 437^48.
322. Reed, T. E., & Jensen, A. R. (1991). Arm nerve conduction velocity (NCV), brain NCV, reaction time, and intelligence. Intelligence, 15, 'i?>-Al.

1992

323. Jensen, A. R. (1992). Understanding g in terms of information processing. Educational Psychology Review, 4, 271-308.
324. Jensen, A. R. (1992). Spearman's hypothesis: Methodology and evidence. Multivariate Behavioral Research, 27, 225-233.
325. Jensen, A. R. (1992). More on Psychometric g and "Spearman's hypothesis." Multivariate Behavioral Research, 27, 257-260.
326. Jensen, A. R. (1992). Scientific fraud or false accusations? The case of Cyril Burt, In: D. J. Miller, & M. Hersen (Eds), Research fraud in the behavioral and biomedical sciences. New York: Wiley & Sons, Inc.
327. Jensen, A. R. (1992). The importance of intraindividual variability in reaction time.
Personality and Individual Differences, 13, 869-882.
328. Jensen, A. R. (1992). Preface. In: R. Pearson (Ed.), Shockley on race, eugenics, and
dysgenics (pp. 1-13). Washington, D.C.: Scott-Townsend.

329. Jensen, A. R. (1992). Mental ability: Critical thresholds and social policy. Journal of Social, Political and Economic Studies, 17, 1-11.
330. Jensen, A. R. (1992). The Cyril Burt scandal, research taboos, and the media. The General Psychologist, 28, 16-21.
331. Jensen, A. R. (1992). The relation between information processing time and right/wrong responses. American Journal on Mental Retardation, 97, 290-292.
332. Jensen, A. R. (1992). Vehicles of g. Psychological Science, 3, 275-278.
333. Jensen, A. R., & Reed, T. E. (1992). The correlation between reaction time and the ponderal index. Perceptual and Motor Skills, 75, 843-846.
334. Jensen, A. R., & Wilson, M. (1992). Henry Felix Kaiser (1927-1992). In Memorium
(pp. 88-91). Berkeley: University of California.
335. Reed, T. E., & Jensen, A. R. (1992). Conduction velocity in a brain nerve pathway of normal adults correlates with intelligence level. Intelligence, 16, 259-278.

1993

336. Jensen, A. R. (1993). Psychometric g and achievement. In: B. R. Gifford (Ed.), Policy perspectives on educational testing (pp. 117-227). Norwell, MA: Kluwer Academic Publishers.
337. Jensen, A. R. (1993). Test validity: g versus "tacit knowledge". Current Directions in Psychological Science, 2, 9-10.
338. Jensen, A. R. (1993). Why is reaction time correlated with psychometric gl Current
Directions in Psychological Science, 2, 53-56.

339. Jensen, A. R. (1993). Spearman's hypothesis tested with chronometric information
processing tasks. Intelligence, 17, 41-17.
340. Jensen, A. R. (1993). Spearman's g: Links between psychometrics and biology. Annals of the New York Academy of Sciences, 702, 103-131.
341. Jensen, A. R., & Sinha, S. N. (1993). Physical correlates of human intelligence. In: P. A. Vernon (Ed.), Biological approaches to the study of human intelligence (pp. 139-242). Norwood, NJ: Ablex.
342. Jensen, A. R., & Whang, P. A. (1993). Reaction times and intelHgence: A comparison of Chinese-American and Anglo-American children. Journal of Biosocial Science, 25, 397-410.
343. Kranzler, J. H., & Jensen, A. R. (1993). Psychometric g is still not unitary after eliminating supposed "impurities": Further comment on Carroll. Intelligence, 17, 11-14.
344. Reed, T. E., & Jensen, A. R. (1993). Choice reaction time and visual pathway nerve
conduction velocity both correlate with intelligence but appear not to correlate with each
other: Implications for information processing. Intelligence, 17, 191-203.
345. Reed, T. E., & Jensen, A. R. (1993). Cranial capacity: New Caucasian data and comments on Rushton's claimed Mongoloid-Caucasoid brain-size differences. Intelligence, 17, 423-431.
346. Reed, T. E., & Jensen, A. R. (1993). A somatosensory latency between the thalamus and cortex also correlates with level of intelligence. Intelligence, 17, 443-450.

1994

347. Jensen, A. R. (1994). Afterword: Deafness and the nature of mental abilities. In: J. P. Braden (Ed.), Deafness, deprivation, and IQ (pp. 203-208). New York: Plenum.
348. Jensen, A. R. (1994). Phlogiston, animal magnetism, and intelligence. In: D. K. Detterman (Ed.), Current topics in human intelligence (Vol. 4): Theories of intelligence (pp. 257-284). Norwood, NJ: Ablex.
349. Jensen, A. R. (1994). Review of "Intelligence" (2nd ed.) by N. Brody. American Journal on Mental Retardation, 98, 663-667.
350. Jensen, A. R. (1994). Reaction time. In: R. J. Corsini (Ed.), Encyclopedia of Psychology (2nd ed., Vol. 3, pp. 282-285). New York: Wiley.
351. Jensen, A. R. (1994). Humphreys's "behavioral repertoire" an epiphenomenon of g. Psychological Inquiry, 5, 208-210.
352. Jensen, A. R. (1994). Francis Galton. In: R. J. Sternberg (Ed.), Encyclopedia of Intelligence (Vol. 1, pp. 457-463). New York: Macmillan.
353. Jensen, A. R. (1994). Charles Edward Spearman. In: R. J. Sternberg (Ed.), Encyclopedia of Intelligence (Vol. 2, pp. 1007-1014). New York: Macmillan.
354. Jensen, A. R. (1994). Hans Jurgen Eysenck. In: R. J. Sternberg (Ed.), Encyclopedia of Intelligence (Vol. 1, pp. 416-418). New York: Macmillan.
355. Jensen, A. R. (1994). Race and IQ scores. In: R. J. Sternberg (Ed.), Encyclopedia of Intelligence (Vol. 2, pp. 899-907). New York: Macmillan.

356. Jensen, A. R. (1994). Psychometric g related to differences in head size. Personality and Individual Differences, 17, 597-606.
357. Jensen, A. R. (1994). Paroxysms of denial. National Review, 46, (Dec. 5), 48-50. (Reprinted in: Jacoby, R., & Glauberman, N. (Eds) (1995), The Bell Curve debate: History, documents, opinion. New York: Random House.
358. Jensen, A. R., & Johnson, F. W. (1994). Race and sex differences in head size and IQ. Intelligence, 18, 309-333.
359. Jensen, A. R., & Ruddell, R. B. (1994). Guy Thomas Buswell. In Memorium (pp. 46-49). Berkeley: University of California.
360. Jensen, A. R., & Weng, J-J. (1994). What is a good gl Intelligence, 18, 231-258.
361. Jensen, A. R., & Whang, P. A. (1994). Speed of accessing arithmetic facts in long-term memory: A comparison of Chinese-American and Anglo-American children. Contemporary Educational Psychology, 19, 1-12.
362. Jensen, A. R., & Wilson, M. (1994). Henry Felix Kaiser (1927-1992) (Obituary). American Psychologist, 49, 1085.
363. Kranzler, J. H., Whang, P. A., & Jensen, A. R. (1994). Task complexity and the speed and efficiency of elemental information processing: Another look at the nature of intellectual giftedness. Contemporary Educational Psychology, 19, 447-459.
364. Shaughnessy, M. F. (1994). An interview with Arthur R. Jensen. The School Field, 4, 129-154.

1995

365. Jensen, A. R. (1995). Psychological research on race differences (Comment). American Psychologist, 50, 41-42.

366. Jensen, A. R. (1995). Wanted: A unified theory of individual and group differences.
(Abstract). Behavior Genetics, 25, 212.
367. Jensen, A. R. (1995). IQ and science: The mysterious Burt affair. In: N. J. Mackintosh (Ed.), Cyril Burt: Fraud or framed? Oxford: Oxford University Press.

1996

368. Jensen, A. R. (1996). Secular trends in IQ: Additional hypotheses. In: D. K. Detterman (Ed.), Current topics in human intelligence (Vol. 4): The environment (pp. 147-150). Norwood, NJ: Ablex.
369. Jensen, A. R. (1996). Inspection Time and g. (Letter), Nature, 381, 729.
370. Jensen, A. R. (1996). The locus of biological g. In: I. Mervielde (Ed.), Abstracts of the 8th European Conference on Personality. University of Ghent, Belgium, July 11, 1996, p. 54.
371. Jensen, A. R. (1996). Giftedness and genius: Crucial differences. In: C. R Benbow, & D. Lubinski (Eds), Intellectual talent: Psychometric and social issues (pp. 393^11).
Baltimore: John Hopkins University Press.
372. Jensen, A. R. (1996). [Review of R. Plomin, "Genetics and experience" (1997)]. Journal of Social and Evolutionary Systems, 19, 307-311. (Reprinted in: European Sociobiological Newsletter, May 1997, No. 44, 24-28).

1997

373. Jensen, A. R. (1997). The puzzle of nongenetic variance. In: R. J. Sternberg & E. L.

Grigorenko (Eds), Intelligence, heredity, and environment (pp. 42-88). Cambridge:
Cambridge University Press.
374. Jensen, A. R. (1997). The neurophysiology oig. In: C. Cooper, & V. Varma (Eds), Processes in individual differences (pp. 108-125). London: Routledge.
375. Jensen, A. R. (1997). Psychometric g and the race question. In: J. Kingma, & W. Tomic (Eds), Reflections on the concept of intelligence (pp. 1-23). Greenwich, CT: JAI Press.
376. Jensen, A. R. (1997). Introduction (to section on intelligence). In: H. Nyborg (Ed.), The scientific study of human nature: Tribute to Hans J. Eysenck at eighty. New York: Elsevier.
377. Jensen, A. R. (1997). The psychometrics of intelligence. In: H. Nyborg (Ed.), The scientific study of human nature: Tribute to Hans J. Eysenck at eighty. New York: Elsevier.
378. Jensen, A. R. (1997). Eysenck as teacher and mentor. In: H. Nyborg (Ed.), The scientific study of human nature: Tribute to Hans J. Eysenck at eighty. New York: Elsevier.

1998

379. Jensen, A. R. (1998). Adoption data and two g-related hypotheses. Intelligence, 25, 1-6.
380. Jensen, A. R. (1998). The g factor Westport, CT: Praeger.
381. Jensen, A. R. (1998). Spearman's law of diminishing returns. In: A. Sen & A. K. Sen (Eds), Challenges of contemporary realities: A psychological perspective (pp. 107-123). New Delhi: New Age International, Ltd.
382. Jensen, A. R. (1998). The g factor in the design of education. In: R. J. Sternberg, & W. M. Williams (Eds),

Intelligence, instruction, and assessment (pp. 111-131). Hillsdale, NJ: Erlbaum.
383. Jensen, A. R. (1998). The suppressed relationship between IQ and the reaction time slope parameter of the Hick function. Intelligence, 26, 43-52.
384. Jensen, A. R. (1998). Jensen on "Jensenism." Intelligence, 26, 181-208.

1999

385. Jensen, A. R. (1999). Review of "Psychological testing of American minorities" by R. J. Samuda. Personality and Individual Differences, 26, 1143-1145.
386. Jensen, A. R. (1999). Review of "InteUigence: A new look" by H. J. Eysenck. The Galton Institute Newsletter, 32, 6-8.
387. Caryl, R G., Deary, I.. J., Jensen, A. R., Neubauer, A. C, & Vickers, D. (1999). Information processing approaches to intelligence: Progress and prospects. In: I. Mervielde, I. Deary, F. de Fruyt, & F. Ostendorf (Eds), Personality Psychology in Europe (Vol. 7, pp. 181-219). Tilburg Univ. Press.

2000

388. Jensen, A. R. (2000). Hans Eysenck's final thoughts on inteUigence. Special review of "InteUigence: A new look" by H. J. Eysenck (1998), Transaction Books. Personality and Individual Differences, 28, 191-194.
389. Jensen, A. R. (2000). Review of "Eminent creativity. Everyday creativity, and health" by M. A. Runco & R. Richards (Eds), Ablex, 1998. Personality and Individual Differences, 28, 198-199.

390. Jensen, A. R. (2000). Elementary cognitive tasks and psychometric g. In: A. Harris (Ed.), Encyclopedia of Psychology. New York: APA/Oxford University Press.
391. Jensen, A. R. (2000). Twins. In: A. Harris (Ed.), Encyclopedia of Psychology. New York: APA/Oxford University Press.
392. Jensen, A. R. (2000). Charles Spearman: Founder of the London School. The Galton
Institute Newsletter, No. 36, 2-4.
393. Jensen, A. R. (2000). Testing: The dilemma of group differences. Psychology, Public Policy and Law, 6, 121-127.
394. Jensen, A. R. (2000). Hans Eysenck: Apostle of the London School. In: G. A. Kimble, & M. Wertheimer (Eds), Portraits of pioneers in psychology (Vol. IV, pp. 338-357). Washington, D.C.: American Psychological Association and Mahwah, NJ: Erlbaum.
395. Jensen, A. R. (2000). Charles Spearman: Discoverer of g. In: G. A. Kimble, & M.
Wertheimer (Eds), Portraits of pioneers in psychology (Vol. IV, pp. 92-111). Washington, D.C.: American Psychological Association and Mahwah, NJ: Erlbaum.
396. Jensen, A. R. (2000). Was wir iiber den ^-Faktor wissen (und nichtwissen). In: K. Schweizer (Ed.), Intelligenze und Kognition: Die kognitiv-biologische Perspektive der Intelligenz (pp. 13-36). Landau: Verlag fiir Empirische Padagogik.
397. Jensen, A. R. (2000). The g factor: Psychometrics and biology (pp. 37-57). Novartis
Foundation Symposium 233. The nature of intelligence. Chichester, England: Wiley.

398. Jensen, A. R. (2000). Some recent overlooked research on the scientific basis of "The Bell Curve." commentary on Reifman on Bell-Curve. Psycoloquy, 11 (106).
399. Jensen, A. R. (2000). "The g factor" is about variance in human abilities, not a cognitive theory of mental structure. Reply to Anderson. Psycoloquy, 11 (041).
400. Jensen, A. R. (2000). A nihilistic philosophy of science for a scientific psychology? Reply to Barrett. Psycoloquy, 11 (088).
401. Jensen, A. R. (2000). Name-caUing is a disappointing substitute for real criticism. Reply to Brace. Psycoloquy, 11, (009).
402. Jensen, A. R. (2000). Artificial intelligence and g theory concern different phenomena. Reply to Bringsjord. Psycoloquy, 11 (086).
403. Jensen, A. R. (2000). The heritability of g proves both its biological relevance and its transcendence over specific cognitive abilities. Reply to Bub. Psycoloquy, 11 (085).
404. Jensen, A. R. (2000). Processing speed, inspection time, and nerve conduction velocity. Reply to Bums. Psycoloquy, 11 (019).
405. Jensen, A. R. (2000). The Ubiquity of mental speed and the centrality of working memory. Reply to Conway et al. Psycoloquy, 11 (038).
406. Jensen, A. R. (2000). Is there a self-awareness of one's own g level? Reply to Demetriou. Psycoloquy, 11 (04).
407. Jensen, A. R. (2000). Mixing up Eugenics and Galton's Legacy to research on inteUigence. Reply to Fancher. Psycoloquy, 11 (017).
408. Jensen, A. R. (2000). Psychometric scepticism. Reply to Harrington. Psycoloquy, 11 (039).

409. Jensen, A. R. (2000). The locus of the modifiability of g is mostly biological. Reply to Hunt. Psycoloquy, 11 (012).
410. Jensen, A. R. (2000). A "simplest cases" approach to exploring the neural basis of ^. Reply to Ingber. Psycoloquy, 11 (023).
411. Jensen, A. R. (2000). A fuzzy boundary of racial classification attenuates IQ difference. Reply to Jorion. Psycoloquy, 11 (022).
412. Jensen, A. R. (2000). A potpourri of ^-related topics. Reply to Kovacs & Pleh. Psycoloquy, 11 (087).
413. Jensen, A. R. (2000). IQ tests, psychometric and chronometric g, and achievement. Reply to Kush. Psycoloquy, 11 (014).
414. Jensen, A. R. (2000). Race differences, g, and the "default hypothesis." Reply to Locurio. Psycoloquy, 11 (004).
415. Jensen, A. R. (2000). Cognitive components as chronometric probes to brain processes. Reply to Mackintosh. Psycoloquy, 11 (Oil).
416. Jensen, A. R. (2000). Behavioral and biological phenomena equally "real" and related. Reply to Partridge. Psycoloquy, 11 (018).
417. Jensen, A. R. (2000). "Biological determinism" as an ideological buzz-word. Reply to Raymond. Psycoloquy, 11 (021).
418. Jensen, A. R. (2000). Nothing 'mystifying' about psychometric g. Reply to Richardson. Psycoloquy, 11 (042).
419. Jensen, A. R. (2000). Correlated vectors, g, and the "Jensen effect". Reply to Rushton. Psycoloquy, 10 (082).
420. Jensen, A. R. (2000). Evoked potentials, testosterone, and g. Reply to Tan. Psycoloquy, 10 (085).

421. Jensen, A. R. (2000). Evoked brain potentials and g. Reply to Verleger. Psycoloquy, 10 (084).
422. Nyborg, H., & Jensen, A. R. (2000). Testosterone levels as modifiers of psychometric g. Personality and individual differences, 28, 601-607.
423. Nyborg, H., & Jensen, A. R. (2000). Black-white differences on various psychometric tests: Spearman's hypothesis tested on American armed services veterans. Personality and Individual Differences, 28, 593-599.

2001
424. Jensen, A. R. (2001). Misleading caricatures of Jensen's statistics: A reply to Kaplan. Chance, 14, 22-26.
425. Jensen, A. R. (2001). Spearman's hypothesis. In: S. Messick, & J. CoUis (Eds), Intelligence and personality: Bridging the gap in theory and measurement (pp. 3-25). Mahwah, NJ: Erlbaum.
426. Jensen, A. R. (2001). Vocabulary and general intelligence. Commentary on Bloom's "How children learn the meanings of words". Behavioral and Brain Sciences, 24, 1109-1110.
427. Nyborg, H., & Jensen, A. R. (2001). Occupation and income related to psychometric g. Intelligence, 29, 45-55.

2002
428. Jensen, A. R. (2002). Gallon's legacy to research on inteUigence (The 1999 Gallon Lecture). Journal of Biosocial Science, 34, 145-172.
429. Jensen, A. R. (2002). Review of Intelligence testing and minority students: Foundations, performance factors, and

assessment issues by R. R. Valencia & L. A. Suzuki (Sage, 2001). Intelligence, 30, 216-217.

430. Jensen, A. R. (2002). General cognitive abiUty (g factor) assessment. In: R. FemandosBallesteros
(Ed.), Encyclopedia of Psychological Assessment. London: Sage.

431. Jensen, A. R. (2002). Psychometric g: Definition and substantiation. In: R. J. Sternberg, &
E. L. Grigorenko (Eds), The g factor: How general is it? Mahwah, NJ: Erlbaum.

In Press

432. Jensen, A. R. (in press). Regularities in Spearman's Law of Diminishing Returns.
Intelligence.

433. Jensen, A. R. (in press). Do age-group differences imitate racial differences? Intelligence.

434. Jensen, A. R. (in press). The mental chronometry of giftedness. In: D. Boothe, & J. C. Stanley (Eds), Giftedness and cultural diversity.

435. Jensen, A. R. (in press). Psychometric g and mental chronometry. Cortex.

436. Jensen, A. R. (in press). Mental chronometry and the unification of differential psychology. In: R. J. Sternberg, & J. Pretz (Eds), Cognition and intelligence. Cambridge: Cambridge University Press.

437. Rushton, J. P., & Jensen, A. R. (in press). African-White IQ differences from Zimbabwe on the Wechsler Scale for Children-Revised. Personality and Individual Differences.

438. Rushton, J. P., & Jensen, A. R. (in press). Thirty Years of research on Black-White
Differences in IQ. Psychology, Public Policy, and Law.

xxi

Index of Exhibits

---

[i] Ruth S. Johnson, *Using Data to Close the Achievement Gap: How to Measure Equity in Our Schools* (Thousand Oaks, CA: Corwin Press, 2002).

[ii] *"Ready to Grow,"* Accenture, Manufacturing Institue, 2014 pg.6.

[iii] http://nces.ed.gov/surveys/pisa/pisa2012/index.asp.

[iv] http://www.payscale.com/cbpr?src=hp_2_cbpr.

[v] *Los Angeles Times*, December 1975.

[vi] "*National Service, Schools,*" TimeMagazine, September 20, 2012, p.35.

[vii] Ruth S. Johnson, *Using Data to Close the Achievement Gap: How to Measure Equity in Our Schools* (Thousand Oaks, CA: Corwin Press, 2002).

[viii] Ruth S. Johnson, *Using Data to Close the Achievement Gap: How to Measure Equity in Our Schools* (Thousand Oaks, CA: Corwin Press, 2002).

[ix] http://www.usa.com/public-school/animo-locke-technology-high-los-angeles-ca-062271011639.html.

---

[x] http://www.greatschools.org/california/los-angeles/10955-Los-Angeles-Center-For-Enriched-Studies/?tab=test-scores.

[xi] Joe Klein, "Learning That Works," Time magazine, May 14, 2012.

[xii] Central Texas Community Dashboards, "% of Youth Who Experience Bullying In School," http://www.centex-communitydashboards.org/Bullying.php.

[xiii] http://whywordshurt.weebly.com/bullying-graphs.html.

[xiv] "*National Service, Schools,*" TimeMagazine, September 20, 2012, p.35.

[xv] *Los Angeles Times*, June 2007

[xvi] Ruth S. Johnson, *Using Data to Close the Achievement Gap: How to Measure Equity in Our Schools* (Thousand Oaks, CA: Corwin Press, 2002).

[xvii] http://www.census.gov/data.html.

---

xviii

http://nces.ed.gov/pubs2007/minoritytrends/tables/table_7_3.asp?referrer=report.

xix Ruth S. Johnson, *Using Data to Close the Achievement Gap: How to Measure Equity in Our Schools* (Thousand Oaks, CA: Corwin Press, 2002).

xx http://www.greatschools.org/california/santa-ana/4065-Arroyo-Elementary-School/details/ http://api.cde.ca.gov/Acnt2014/apiavgsch.aspx?allcds=30736436030548.

Our Education System

"Everybody is a genius. But if you judge a fish by its ability to climb a tree, it will live its whole life believing that it is stupid."

- Albert Einstein